C Notes

A Guide to the
C Programming Language

By C.T. Zahn

YOURDON Press
1133 Avenue of the Americas
New York, New York 10036

Our thanks to Chilton Book Co. for permission to reprint the quotation on p. 33 from *Dune* by Frank Herbert. Copyright © 1965 by Chilton Book Co.

Printed in the United States of America

ISBN: 0-917072-13-8

Library of Congress Catalog Number 78-63290

This book was set in Times Roman by YOURDON Press, using a PDP-11/45 running under the UNIX operating system.

CONTENTS

PREFACE

C is a language that is rapidly growing in popularity. From quiet beginnings in the attic of Bell Labs, Murray Hill, it has spread to hundreds of machines all over the world; and it has done so with little or no sales effort.

C can be described as an implementable Algol 68, or as a Pascal that's not afraid to get its hands dirty, or simply as an elegant little language that meets the needs of system-level programmers. None of these views captures the full import of the *balance* that has been so carefully struck between purity and practicality, between portability and efficiency.

The language C has been designed to provide maximum function with minimum form. The purpose of this book is to provide a guide to the language, a guide that is formally precise yet that does not hesitate to elucidate the darker corners of implementation dependencies and semantic peculiarities. It is not a tutorial — one cannot compete with Kernighan and Ritchie's *The C Programming Language* — nor is it a formal definition: Appendix A of their book serves well enough for that. Rather, it fills in the middle ground and provides a perspective on C that differs from the Bell Labs view. As implementations proliferate, that broader perspective will become progressively more important.

This is a two-dimensional book. The chapters cover the gross aspects of the language:

0. Syntax

1. External declarations

2. Initializers and statements

3.   Expressions

4.   Local declarations

5.   Parameterization

6.   Library routines

7.   Machine dependencies

Each chapter consists of eight sections visiting the various data types:

.0   Introduction

.1   Integers

.2   Floating numbers

.3   Pointers

.4   Arrays

.5   Structures and unions

.6   Functions

.7   Summary

To get a quick overview of the language, read the .0 sections of each of the chapters; to get a precise summary, read the .7 sections. Everything peculiar to, say, pointers can be found in the .3 sections, and pointer expressions are surely discussed in Chapter 3, .3 section, or [3.3] for short.

The language described here adheres closely to the specifications promulgated by Dennis Ritchie in the aforementioned Appendix A. It should be emphasized, however, that *none* of the existing compilers match that specification precisely, although C is still rather pure.

0: SYNTAX

What do you read, my Lord?
Words, words, words.

— Shakespeare, *Hamlet*

0.0 Introduction

The C programming language consists of a language definition, an implementation, and a run-time environment. The language definition describes C independent of any particular machine characteristics; the implementation strives to enforce that definition in terms of some real computer; and the corresponding run-time environment makes up for any inadequacies in the implementation or in the machine, in order to emulate an abstract *C machine* with sufficient fidelity to satisfy the language definition.

C is a machine-independent language that attempts to model the basic operators and operands of most modern computers. As such, C is capable of being translated into efficient and compact code on a variety of machines, but only at the cost of a certain amount of indeterminacy in the language definition. It is necessary, therefore, to occasionally stress those aspects of a C program that may vary among different implementations; and it often is useful to know what can be controlled by mere changes in the run-time support package.

This book will focus primarily on the machine-independent definition of C, since that is its most portable aspect. But it is important to keep in mind that C is implemented as a *compiler*,

1

that is, a program written in C that reads programs written in C and writes out assembly language statements to implement the intent of the source code. The *assembler* translates these statements into an object module, a collection of instructions to a *loader*, which actually constructs the executable program. The loader may combine the object module with other separately compiled and/or assembled modules, and it may draw upon a library of run-time support routines to complete the program. Many of the high-handed limitations imposed by C compilers are simply a reflection of the inadequacies common to most assemblers and/or loaders.

A C program is a set of one or more text files — each of which can be, say, a paper tape or a deck of cards or an on-line file prepared with a text editor. It consists of lines of arbitrary length, each of which is terminated by a special character code called *newline* (ASCII linefeed). The run-time environment translates standard text files into this internal format for the compiler, if need be, so that the concept of line can be implemented in a uniform fashion across different operating systems and machines. A card image, for example, might become an 81-character line, counting the terminating newline.

Here is a not-unreasonable C program:

```
/* copy input to output
*/
main( )
        {
        int c;

        c = getchar( );
        while (c != -1)
                {
                putchar(c);
                c = getchar( );
                }
        }
```

This declares **main** to be a function, called with no arguments, whose body is the text inside braces. The body declares **c** to be an integer variable known only to the function, and contains several executable statements which call on other functions **getchar** and **putchar** repeatedly until **c** is given the value −**1**. It turns out that these other functions are available on the run-time library (see [6.0]); there is nothing otherwise magical about them.

Clearly, a lot more explanation is in order, but that must be spread over several chapters. For now, the focus must remain on the building blocks of a C program, how it is expressed, and the basic data with which it deals. At the lowest level, it consists of various *identifiers*, or names, interspersed with literals, punctuation, and *whitespace*, e.g. blanks and tabs.

C programs are written using the full set (see [7.1]) of 94 printable ASCII characters. Contiguous strings of printable characters are lumped into *tokens* according to various lexical rules. All nonprinting characters, including newline, are whitespace, which is used to separate adjacent tokens that might otherwise be lumped together. There also are *comments*, arbitrary strings of characters that begin with /* and end with */, which behave much like whitespace. Although the language imposes few constraints on the use of whitespace or comments, it is imperative that both be employed judiciously and uniformly to make source code as readable as possible.

Identifiers are arbitrary-length strings of letters, digits, and the underscore character _, beginning with a letter or the underscore character. The C program shown on the previous page contains the identifiers **main**, **int**, **c**, **getchar**, **while**, and **putchar**. Names that are used by the loader (see [7.0]) all must differ in the first five or so characters (depending on the particular loader) to be distinguishable; internally used names must differ in the first eight characters. Some loaders refuse to distinguish between uppercase and lowercase letters. Identifiers generally are created by the user to name data items and functions.

Certain identifiers are predefined *keywords*, each having special meaning in the language; they may not be redefined. In the example above, **int** and **while** are keywords. A complete list of keywords may be found in [0.7]. Since lowercase and uppercase letters are distinct in full ASCII, **INT** is not a keyword, nor is **Int**. Installations that support uppercase-only devices must translate to lowercase on input to the compiler, and possibly back to uppercase on output.

All other printable characters, besides those used to construct identifiers, are considered punctuation and are used to construct operators, delimiters, and (in part) literals. In the example, =, !=, and − are operators; (,), {, }, and ; are delimiters. Tokens constructed from punctuation are all predefined in C. A complete list of operators and delimiters may be found at the end of the chapter, in [0.7].

Operators and delimiters may be run together, with no intervening whitespace. When this occurs, the longest identifiable token is taken as the prefix of the punctuation string, regardless of any contextual information that might suggest a happier division. Thus, it is good practice to delimit most adjacent operators with whitespace, since these often are easily confused by both reader and compiler.

The remaining class of tokens is literals, which come in several flavors. In the example above, **1** is an integer literal, a decimal number with a value of one. Other literals are character **'x'**, octal **017**, hexadecimal **0X1FF**, long **13L**, floating **3.07**, and string **"help!"**. The flavors are closely allied with the notion of data types, which is the subject of the rest of this chapter. Each of the literals will be discussed in conjunction with its corresponding data type, and will be summarized in [0.7].

All objects comprising a C program have one set of attributes that determines where the object is to be found, and another set that determines its size, shape, and the allowable operations that can be performed upon it. The first set of attributes is called *storage class*, the second is *type*. This chapter will confine itself to objects of what could be called the *immediate* storage class, represented by the various literals, in the process of introducing each of the types. Later chapters will introduce the declarable storage classes one or two at a time.

The types, in the order they will be treated in each chapter, are: *integer*, which also includes *character*, *short integer*, *unsigned integer*, and *long integer; floating*, which also includes *double; pointer; array; structure*, which includes *union;* and *function*. In the example, **main, getchar,** and **putchar** are functions; **c** and **1** are integers, as are the values returned by all the functions.

The types can be classified as *fundamental* (integer and floating) versus *derived* (pointer, array, structure, union, function), or as *scalar* (fundamental plus pointer) versus *composite* (array, structure, union, function).

A summary of the types will be given in [0.7].

0.1 Integers

Integers are the workhorses of a C program. They are used for counting, for selecting elements of an array, for representing characters of text, logical values, and bit sequences, and for any arithmetic where the magnitude range is known to be limited and fractional results are not needed. It is no surprise that integers are implemented in a wide variety of ways.

The basic integer can be represented as a binary datum, although there is no presumption in the language about whether arithmetic is performed in one's complement, two's complement, signed magnitude, or some more exotic encoding. Integers in C always will be at least as big as are addresses on the target machine; they can be used unreservedly as subscripts or pointer modifiers.

Short integers can be used, in the hope of achieving storage economy, for counting things in the thousands. There is no guarantee, however, that a short integer actually will be any shorter than a basic integer. Similarly, long integers are used for counting things in the hundreds of millions; they also may be no longer than basic integers.

Unsigned integers are typically the same size as basic integers and behave much the same in arithmetic, except that their values are always taken as zero or positive. On two's complement computers, this has the net effect of treating the sign bit as just another magnitude bit. Their primary use is not so much to double the range of counting with positive numbers as to permit arithmetic that is compatible with the treatment of addresses on machines where an address fills up an integer-sized word.

Finally, C provides a *character* type that is guaranteed to be large enough to hold any element of the machine's character set. Characters behave like very small integers when used in arithmetic expressions, but there is no guarantee that negative numbers will survive conversion to character and back to integer, no matter how small they are. It can be safely assumed that the printing characters behave like small positive numbers.

This discussion so far has been evasive about actual data sizes, and intentionally so. C does know about *bytes*, in the usual machine sense, and even about *bits* to a much lesser extent. The point is, considerable variation is permitted in implementation sizes, so that C can be made to perform efficiently on an Intel 8080 or an IBM 370. All that is really promised has been summarized in the paragraphs above.

Most modern computers have eight-bit bytes, support data types that are multiples of bytes, and perform integer arithmetic in two's complement. On such machines, one can reliably expect characters to fit in one byte and integers in two to four. Thus, a character may hold numbers in the range -128 to $+127$, or perhaps 0 to 255; two-byte integers are $-32,768$ to $+32,767$ signed, or 0 to 65,535 unsigned; and four-byte integers are $-2,147,483,648$ to $+2,147,483,647$ signed or 0 to 4,294,967,295 unsigned. The size of addresses, in bytes, will give a good indication of whether basic integers are on the short or long side of that range. It is perfectly legal, of course, for *all* integers, to be four bytes long.

A good program will be written with the fewest wired-in assumptions about the nature of the target machine, so as to maximize portability and to minimize mysterious constants. To aid in portability, C provides a mechanism for determining the size of any data type, expressed in bytes, so that the code can be properly parameterized. The **sizeof** operator is described in [3.1].

Integer literals may be expressed several different ways. Each implies by its form and value some minimum length, in bytes, which may affect how it is used in expressions, although an implementation may use a longer version than is required.

Any literal beginning with a nonzero digit and consisting only of digits is taken as a *decimal* integer. Its length is the minimum implemented type large enough to let it be represented as a *positive* number of the correct value.

A literal beginning with the digit zero, **0**, and consisting only of digits is taken as an *octal* integer. The digit eight, **8**, is taken as octal 10, and nine, **9**, is taken as octal 11. The length of the literal is the minimum implemented type large enough to let it be represented as an *unsigned* number of the correct value.

A literal beginning with the digit zero followed by x or **X** is taken as a *hexadecimal* integer. The characters **a** through **f**, or equally **A** through **F**, are taken as hexadecimal digits with values ten through fifteen, respectively. The length of the literal is the minimum type large enough to let it be represented as an *unsigned* number of the correct value.

A literal beginning with a single quote, ', is taken as a *character* integer. All characters, including whitespace, up to the next single quote are taken as literal characters that define the value of the integer. A single character is the length of a character datum and has a value equal to the internal representation of that character on the target machine. Additional characters are concatenated in unspecified order, giving a length that is the appropriate multiple of a single character.

Certain nonprinting or difficult-to-obtain characters may be represented by an *escape sequence,* such as \n for newline or \' for single quote, since neither of these may otherwise occur within a string. Arbitrary codes may be specified with \nnn, where *nnn* is one to three octal digits. Note that all of these escape sequences reduce to single characters in the constant. A complete list of escape sequences for characters may be found in [0.7]. If it is necessary to continue a character literal on a subsequent line, the escape \ may be used right before a newline to nullify its effect.

Despite all this freedom, it is wise to restrict character literals severely. Literals with more than one character are extremely machine-dependent, and literals with nonprinting characters are difficult to check. Escape sequences should be used to make all codes visible, and line continuation should be avoided. And, while character literals are truly integers and can be used freely in integer expressions, it is best not to presume any specific numeric values or ranges, since both may vary from one machine to another. Character literals should be used primarily for output or for exact comparisons with character data.

Any integer literal may have the modifier l or, far preferably, L appended to it. This forces the length to be that of a long integer, regardless of its numeric value. If any integer literal is too long to be properly represented even as a long integer, it is taken as long and is truncated on the left. What happens to the sign is machine-dependent.

0.2 Floating numbers

A *floating number* has two elements: an exponent and a fractional part. Its value is interpreted as the product of the fractional part and some predefined base raised to the exponent power. At least one coding of exponent and fractional part is used to represent the value zero. Floating numbers can be considered as approximations to the real number set over a range that is large compared to the range of integers.

Floating point arithmetic can maintain a fixed amount of precision over this large range, at the expense of representing very large integers or continued fractions inexactly. Numbers too large to be represented properly as floating are said to *overflow;* numbers too small *underflow*, and are usually approximated by zero. Subtracting two numbers with nearly equal magnitudes can cause *significance loss*, so that only a coarse approximation to the desired result is obtained.

Despite these drawbacks, floating arithmetic is so popular for numeric calculations that most modern computers support some version of it with hardware instructions. Whether results are rounded, truncated, or approximated more haphazardly varies wildly among machines. As a consequence, C has little to say about the detailed properties of floating arithmetic.

The language does, however, provide the data types *floating* and *double*. Despite the name, there is no guarantee that a double-precision floating number has a fractional part twice as long as a basic floating datum. It is often *more* than twice as long, but it also may be no longer than a float. Nor is there any guarantee that any particular length integer can be *widened* to float and then converted back to an integer having the same value, even though the double representation is presumed to retain the most information of all arithmetic types.

On most machines, floating data are represented in four to eight bytes, a fixed part of which is used to represent the exponent. The implied base in binary computers is usually either two or sixteen; magnitudes typically range up to ten to the 38th power, at least; and fractional parts retain from six to sixteen decimal digits of precision.

Floating literals are tokens that begin with either a decimal number or a decimal point. They may contain a decimal point, a fractional part, and an exponent part, where the exponent part consists of the character e or E, an optional plus or minus sign, and a decimal power of ten by which the rest of the number is multiplied. Either the integer part or the fractional part may be omitted, but not both; either the decimal point or the exponent may be omitted, but not both. No whitespace may occur between any of the parts of a floating literal.

There is no special notation for a double literal, but sufficient precision is retained to generate a double constant should the context call for one. A literal of sufficient specified precision always will be taken as double. Default typing of floating literals is discussed in [3.2].

0.3 Pointers

Pointers are data items that are used to locate other data items. In the simplest implementation, a pointer simply holds the machine address of the datum pointed to; but it could, in principle, hold a more elaborate construct, such as a word address plus a byte offset, or a reference count to facilitate validity checking and garbage collection. A pointer must at least be big enough to hold the largest machine address usable in a program.

What is important is that pointers are characterized by the sort of thing they point to; there is no such thing in C as a pointer to unspecified type. Pointers to different types of things may well have different formats; almost certainly there are different constraints on the values they may take on. For all pointers, however, there is defined a *null* value, distinguishable from the address of any object in C, which the pointer may take on when it points to no current instance of the appropriate type.

It is permissible to have pointers to any type of object in C, including to other pointers, recursively ad nauseam. They arise naturally in many aspects of programming, but are most particularly useful in contexts in which the object itself should not or cannot be conveyed directly. It is much easier, for instance, to deliver to some function a copy of a pointer than to copy an entire array or data structure. And, it is not possible to represent some list structures unless pointers can be used to stand for sublists: Consider a circular list, for instance, in which each element is in its own sublist.

It is also possible to abuse pointers, since they introduce a level of indirection that obscures readability, and since they provide a degree of programming freedom that is almost impossible to check thoroughly at compile-time or efficiently at run-time. C allows considerable latitude in the use of pointers, at the expense of even some checking that is easy to perform. Consequently, they should be used with particular care.

There are no pointer literals, per se, in the language. It is promised, however, that *all* valid pointers have nonzero values, so that an integer zero can serve as a literal null. Moreover, integers can be used in a variety of contexts to initialize pointers, although this practice is *extremely* machine-dependent.

0.4 Arrays

Any object of known size in C also can occur in multiples, known as *arrays*. Like a pointer *to* something, an array is always *of* some other type, although that type also can be an array of still other types. There is no explicit limit to the *dimensionality* of an array, just as there is no limit to the length of a chain of pointers. An array of arrays of pointers to arrays of integers is quite acceptable.

An array also is characterized by its starting address and by the number of elements it contains, that is, its *multiplicity*. The former is determined by its storage class, and must have a value that is legal for pointers to objects of the same type as the elements of the array. In this sense, an array starting address can be considered a literal pointer.

C has no provision for variable-length arrays, although a program is of course at liberty to use less than the full multiplicity of elements in an array. This means that in many contexts the number of elements must be determined before an array can be referred to, and that there is no information stored with an array other than the current values of all its elements. Some latitude is permitted in determining the multiplicity, so that the compiler often can be made to count up things itself instead of burdening the programmer. It is illegal for an array to have a multiplicity of zero.

An array with undetermined multiplicity is not "an object of known size" and hence may not be composed into other arrays or used in one or two other contexts. It also is not permissible to form an array of functions, or of structures whose contents are not determined.

There is one kind of literal array. A literal that begins with a double quote, ", is taken as a *character string*, or array of characters. All characters following the double quote, including whitespace, up to the next double quote are taken as character integers that define succeeding elements of an array of characters. A null character, \0, is appended to every string, so that a character string always has a multiplicity of at least one, as in "", which is the null string.

The same escape sequences defined for character integers in [0.1] and [0.7] are usable inside strings. In particular, \" is a literal double quote, \\ is a literal backslash, and \ newline continues the string on the next line. The style rules pertaining to character integers also should be applied.

0.5 Structures and unions

Often, data items of differing types want to be grouped together because the items are strongly related. Input-output records are a typical example of aggregates, as are complex numbers. The former can be, and often is, represented as an array of characters, but that disguises the relationship among characters of a particular subfield. Similarly, the latter can be considered a two-element array of floats, if one ignores the asymetry in processing the two fields. It is far more general, however, to provide for aggregates of arbitrary types; this is the purpose of data structures in C.

Any objects of known size can be collected into a *structure,* including pointers, arrays, or other structures. A structure is defined by the order and types of its elements; two structures match only if their corresponding elements have the same types collected in the same order. No information regarding the composition of a structure is stored with it, just the values of each of its elements.

There can be regions of program text in which a given structure can be referred to before its contents are defined. In this region, the structure is not an object of known size, and hence cannot be composed into arrays or other structures.

It is tempting to think that the size of a structure is the sum of the size of each of its elements, but this is naive. Many modern computers have some restrictions on the placement of certain data types in storage. A four-byte floating datum may, for instance, be required to have a machine address that is exactly divisible by four. Thus, each data type is characterized not only by its size in bytes but also by the severity of its storage boundary restrictions.

The obvious consideration inside a structure is that an element might not be placeable immediately after the previous element — holes may occur, the size and location of which are machine-dependent. It is equally clear that a structure itself must be aligned on a storage boundary at least as restrictive as that needed for its most restricted element. Thus, if a four-byte float were to follow a character, for instance, it is conceivable that a three-byte hole would have to be introduced. If floats were required to begin on even addresses, as in the PDP-11, then a one-byte hole would occur.

A more subtle requirement is that a structure must *end* on a boundary at least as restricted as that on which it begins. This is to ensure that an array of structures will meet all boundary requirements for elements after the first. So a structure may even have a hole on the end, as it were.

There are no structure literals.

A close relative of the data structure is the *union* of types. Unions occur frequently in programs where more than one type of data must be placed in the same storage location. Often the overlap takes advantage of known similarities in sizes of the different types to be used, and possibly in how they are moved about; this is extremely machine-dependent. Like using an array to represent a structure, it can be misleading as well.

Any objects of known size can be collected into a union, whose size is then large enough to hold the largest of its elements and whose boundary restriction is as severe as the severest of its elements. Like a structure, a union also may be padded so that it ends on the same boundary as that on which it must begin. Unlike a structure, only one of the choice of elements may reside inside a union at any given moment. No information regarding the composition of a union, or the type of its current contents, is stored with it — just the value of one of its elements.

Thus, unions are used primarily to inform the implementation of a practice that is very likely to be machine-dependent, so that the compiler can meet the minimum requirements of whatever target machine is chosen.

There are no union literals.

0.6 Functions

Functions are the executable entities of C. They may represent compound actions to be performed, or call for the calculation of mathematical functions of one or more arguments.

Each C program must contain a function named **main**, whose single performance defines the execution of the program. Such a program has been described in [0.0].

Just as pointers always are declared as *pointing to* some known type, functions always are declared as *returning* some type, even if no type is explicitly mentioned (see [1.6]), no value is explicitly returned [2.6], or no returned value is ever used [3.6]. Functions may only return scalar types, i.e., integers, floats, or pointers.

Arguments to functions are passed by *value*, i.e. a fresh copy of each argument is made for each invocation of the function, and the function is at liberty to alter these private copies. As with returned values, only scalar types may be passed as arguments (but see [3.4, 3.5, 3.6] for implicit coercion of non-scalars to scalars).

Although a valid C program can consist of the **main** function alone, it is usual to delegate a number of the activities required by **main** to other functions and to continue this process until the functions are all of a manageable size. The communication between **main** and its subordinate functions is accomplished normally by a list of arguments and possibly by a result returned. In other cases, functions can communicate implicitly by common access to globally known variables, although this leads to less readable programs.

The following three functions, named **main**, **newnum**, and **printd**, illustrate the major possibilities:

```
int c;     /* globally known current input character */
main( )     /* read, convert, and print number */
    {
    int number;
    c = getchar( );
    number = 0;
    while (isdigit(c))
        {
        number = newnum(number);
        c = getchar( );
        }
    printd(number);
    }
```

```
int newnum(n)     /* fold digit c into n */
    int n;
    {
    return (10 * n + (c - '0'));
    }

printd(n)     /* print n as decimal */
    int n;
    {
    int quot, rem;

    quot = n / 10;
    rem = n % 10;
    if (quot != 0)
            printd(quot);     /* recursive call */
    putchar(rem + '0');
    }
```

In the example, **main**, **newnum**, and **printd**, as well as a global integer **c**, keep the current character just read from input. The function **main** employs a library function **getchar** and three others to discharge its duties. Two of these are defined here; **isdigit** remains to be defined.

The function **newnum** performs a calculation based on the explicitly denoted argument **n** and the implicit global argument **c**; since **newnum** returns a result of type integer, it is called from within an expression in **main**. It should be emphasized, however, that this method of passing **c** to the function **newnum** is odious in most cases.

The function **printd** does not return a value; it is invoked for the actions it performs, namely to print a sequence of digits on the output medium. Hence, the call from **main** to **printd** occurs as a statement rather than from inside an expression. Had **printd** been defined as returning a result, the call in **main** would still be legal but the returned value would be discarded and never used. This function differs from the others in that it delegates certain duties to itself via the call **printd(quot)**. Such *recursive* calls are generally allowed in C, but the programmer must carefully avoid infinite recursion.

A function is not an object of known size, and hence may not be composed into arrays, structures, or unions. It is perfectly legal, however, for *pointers to functions* to be so used.

There are no literal function values, although the formal arguments and the function body are tantamount to that. These topics are discussed in greater detail in [2.6], which deals with function initializers.

0.7 Syntax summary

A properly formed C program consists of a sequence of tokens grouped into phrases in a very precise way. The rules prescribing the set of properly formed C programs are known as the *syntax*. Each rule defines the meaning of a particular *phrase name* by specifying all possible ways of building such a phrase from primitive tokens and other phrases. The first rule defines the phrase "C program" as a sequence of one or more program files and is written:

$$C\text{-}program = \{ \ program\text{-}file \}$$

The braces imply one or more occurrences.

Another rule defines a type definition as the keyword **typedef**, followed by a type specifier followed by a declarator list, followed by the token ; .

This rule is written:

$$type\text{-}definition =$$
$$\textbf{typedef} \ \ type\text{-}specifier \ declarator\text{-}list \ ;$$

The phrase type specifier is defined by

$$type\text{-}specifier =$$
$$[\ integer\text{-}type \ | \ floating\text{-}type$$
$$| \ type\text{-}name \ | \ structure\text{-}or\text{-}union\text{-}type \ ]$$

which means a choice of one of the four alternatives. A subscript *opt* indicates optional occurrence so that

$$floating\text{-}type =$$
$$[\ \textbf{short}_{opt} \ \ \textbf{double} \ | \ \textbf{long}_{opt} \ \textbf{float} \ ]$$

means the keyword **double**, possibly preceded by **short**, or else **float**, possibly preceded by **long**. Occasionally, parentheses are used to group a sequence of phrases that is optional as in

$$(\ \textbf{else} \ statement \ )_{opt}$$

Keywords of C and other literal tokens are in boldface while phrase names are italicized with imbedded hyphens. Any phrase name of the form *anything-list* is an abbreviation for a comma-separated sequence of one or more phrases of the *anything* variety. The formal meaning could be given by the following schema:

> *anything-list* =   % *this is a comment*
>   *anything* { , *anything* }$_{opt}$

As shown above, syntax comments may be inserted into the formal syntax rules after a percent sign and before the next newline.

Occasionally, one of the alternatives in an optional choice will have the subscript *def* to indicate that, if the phrase is missing, the interpretation will be just as if that choice had been explicitly given. Such implicit choices are known as *defaults*. A typical example in C is

> [**auto**$_{def}$| **static** | **extern** | **register**]$_{opt}$

The following rules specify the lexical format of the tokens of C programs:

> *identifier* =
>   [*letter* | _] { [*letter* | _ | *digit*] }$_{opt}$
>
> *keyword* =
>   [**auto** | **break** | **case** | **char** | **continue**
> | **default** | **do** | **double** | **else** | **extern**
> | **float** | **for** | **goto** | **if** | **int** | **long**
> | **register** | **return** | **short** | **sizeof** | **static**
> | **struct** | **switch** | **typedef** | **union**
> | **unsigned** | **while**]
>
> *comment* =
>   /* *character-sequence-not-containing-asterisk-slash* */
>
> *integer-constant* =
>   [*decimal-constant* | *octal-constant*
> | *hexadecimal-constant* | *character-constant*]

decimal-constant =
     nonzero-digit { *digit* }$_{opt}$

octal-constant =
     0 { *digit* }

hexadecimal-constant =
     0 *[* **x** *|* **X** *]* { *hex-digit* }$_{opt}$

hex-digit =
     [digit | **a** *|* **b** *|* **c** *|* **d** *|* **e** *|* **f**
     | **A** *|* **B** *|* **C** *|* **D** *|* **E** *|* **F** *]*

floating-constant =
     [[decimal-constant | **0** *] . decimal-constant*$_{opt}$ *exponent*$_{opt}$
     | . decimal-constant exponent$_{opt}$
     | [decimal-constant | **0** *] exponent]*

fraction =
     . decimal-constant$_{opt}$

exponent =
     [**e** *|* **E** *] [* **+** *|* **−** *]*$_{opt}$ *decimal-constant*

character-constant =
     ' { *character-literal* }$_{opt}$ **'**

string =
     " { *character-literal* }$_{opt}$ **"**

character-literal =
     [character-other-than-\-"-or-'
     | **\b**   % *backspace*
     | **\n**   % *newline*
     | **\r**   % *carriage return*
     | **\t**   % *tab character*
     | ****   % *backslash*
     | **\"**   % **"**
     | **\'**   % **'**
     | *****octal-digit*
     | *****octal-digit octal-digit*
     | *****octal-digit octal-digit octal-digit*
     ]

punctuation =
     [**(|** **)**   % *grouping and association*
     | **[|** **]**   % *array subscripts*
     | **{ |** **}**   % *initializers and compound statements*
     | **, |** **;**   % *separators and terminators*
     | **? |** **:**   % *conditional expressions*
     ]

operator =
    [*arithmetic-operator*
    | *bitwise-operator*
    | *parts-selection-operator*
    | *dereferencing-operator*
    | *location-operator*
    | *logical-operator*
    | *augmentation-operator*
    | *relational-operator*
    | *equality-operator*
    ]

arithmetic-operator =
    [+ | − | * | / | %]

bitwise-operator =
    [& | | | ^ | << | >> | ~]

parts-selection-operator =
    [. | −>]

dereferencing-operator =
    *

location-operator =
    &

logical-operator =
    [&& | || | !]

augmentation-operator =
    [++ | −−]

relational-operator =
    [< | > | <= | >=]

equality-operator =
    [== | !=]

1: EXTERNAL DECLARATIONS

"When I use a word," Humpty Dumpty said, in
rather a scornful tone, *"it means just what I choose
it to mean — neither more nor less."*

— Lewis Carroll, *Through the Looking-glass*

1.0 Global declarations

A *C program* consists of a sequence of one or more
separately compiled files. A *program file* is a sequence of
function declarations, type definitions, and *data declarations.* This is
specified more formally by the rules:

C-program = { program-file }

*program-file =
    { [function-declaration | type-definition
    | data-declaration] }*

It is important to recognize that a C program is *nothing but* declarations at the outermost or external level, and that *all* expressions and statements in the language serve merely as initializers
for some item being declared.

The further description of the syntax and meaning of these
forms of external, or global, declaration is the task of this
chapter. In simplest terms, a declaration introduces some variable and associates various attributes with it.

A program dealing exclusively with constants is usually not
of great usefulness; so the concept of *variable* has taken on great
significance for most programming languages, and C is no exception. A simple variable is a pair consisting of a *name* and an *object;* the name is an identifier required by the programmer to

specify which objects are to be manipulated, while each object consists of a *location* (usually a computer address and size), a type, and a particular value of that type stored at the location.

The reason for being so careful with the terminology is that when pointers and composite types are encountered later, there will emerge variables with more complicated name expressions, and the syntax and meaning of the well-known assignment will require careful consideration. There also is an operator in the language that delivers the location of a variable, thereby making the computer address a manipulatable value. A correct understanding of pointers also must be based on a clear understanding of variables.

The external declarations announce certain names as having attributes desired by the programmer. For example,

```
int i;
long float x;
```

gives the name i the attribute of variable-with-integer-type (the implementation takes care of the actual location), and x becomes a variable of type double-precision floating.

In addition to types, a declaration can also specify a storage class attribute and an initializer. Initializers will be introduced in Chapter 2. The storage class, if present, must be written first:

```
static int i;
extern long float x;
```

Storage classes are specified by the keywords **extern**, **static**, **auto**, and **register**; the **typedef** specifier behaves syntactically like a storage class, but does not associate a name with an object.

Every externally declared name in a C program file has either the external or static attribute, denoted by the keywords **extern** and **static**, external being the default. An external name is visible in all program files, and this facility allows communication between separately compiled program files. A static name is visible throughout the remainder of the enclosing program file but not more widely. The use of separate program files and restricted use of the external attribute can provide modularity and protection not provided by some languages.

Globally declared variables have a lifetime that endures for as long as the main program executes regardless of their visibility attribute (external or static).

Sections [1.1] through [1.5] deal with the various kinds of *data-declarations,* so it is appropriate to introduce the formal syntax rules here:

data-declaration =
   [**extern**$_{def}$| **static**]$_{opt}$
   type-specifier$_{opt}$ *initializable-declarator-list*$_{opt}$;

type-specifier =
   [*integer-type*| *floating-type*
   | *type-name*| *structure-or-union-type*]

initializable-declarator =
   declarator initializer$_{opt}$

Function-declarations will be covered in [1.6], and *type-definitions* at the end of the chapter, in [1.7].

1.1 Integer declarations

An external *integer declaration* is a data declaration with a type specifier of the flavor integer type:

integer-type =
   [**char**| [**unsigned**| **short**| **long**]$_{opt}$ **int**$_{def}$]

and declarators that are identifiers. The declaration

int number, smallest, largest;

makes **number, smallest,** and **largest** the names of three integer variables, which are externally visible by default. Any subsequent reference to one of these names will deliver its current value or cause replacement of its current value by a new value, depending on the context in which the name occurs.

These integer variables can participate as operands of integer operators, as described in [3.1]. The various flavors of integer type were explained in [0.1].

If any of the adjectives **short, unsigned,** or **long** is present, **int** is assumed and may be omitted. In any context calling for an optional type specifier, the default type is taken as **int**. It is good practice, however, to explicitly type *all* declarations.

1.2 Floating declarations

An external *floating declaration* is a data declaration with a type specifier of the flavor floating type:

floating-type =
[short$_{opt}$ **double** | **long**$_{opt}$ **float**]

and declarations which are identifiers. For example,

static long float x;
float y;

makes **x** the name of a floating variable of long precision, visible only in the enclosing program file, and **y** an externally visible single-precision floating variable. They may participate in expressions much as integers do, but with slightly different meaning attached to the operators. The operators relevant to floating variables are described in [3.2].

1.3 Pointer declarations

An external *pointer declaration* is a data declaration with any flavor of type specifier and a declaration of the form

* *declarator*

For example,

int *ptr_to_int;
struct item **ptr_to_item;

declares **ptr_to_int** as the name of a variable of type pointer to integer and **ptr_to_item** as a variable of type pointer to a pointer to the structured type **struct item**. The structured type **struct item** is a composite type whose definition presumably occurs elsewhere, but note that the content of the structure need not be known to declare a pointer to it.

Recalling the earlier definition of variable, the unique aspect of a pointer variable is that its class of admissible values ranges over the locations (machine addresses) of other variables of the type to which the pointer variable is specified to point. The use of these variables will be described subsequently in several chapters.

1.4 Array declarations

An external *array declaration* is a data declaration with any type specifier and a declaration of the form

$$\textit{identifier} \; [\; \textit{constant-expr}_{opt} \;]$$

The *constant-expr* must be a positive integer constant, calculable at compile-time, and defines the multiplicity N of the array. The valid subscripts range from 0 to N−1. For example,

float point_3d[3];

declares **point_3d** as an array variable consisting of three subvariables **point_3d[0]**, **point_3d[1]**, and **point_3d[2]** each of type **float**. The expressions **point_3d[2]**, **point_3d[k]**, and **point_3d[j−2]** are *variable-name-exprs,* each of which refers to one of the three floating variables making up the composite floating array variable **point_3d**.

The *constant-expr* specifying array size may be omitted when an initializer is present and the size is implied by the number of values supplied. Initializers for arrays are discussed in [2.4]. It also is permissible to omit the size when declaring the existence of an array that is defined elsewhere, perhaps in another program file. It is possible to declare variables that are arrays of arrays, and so on, as in

char page[50][80];

which makes **page** the name of an array variable composed of **50** like variables of size **80** characters. Then **page[0][0]** and **page[49][79]** denote the northwest and southeast corners, respectively. When a declaration contains array of array, and so forth, only the first size specification may be omitted, for otherwise the contained arrays would not be objects of known size.

The character strings described in [0.4] are literal arrays of characters and behave like **char** array names, except when used as initializers of named **char** arrays. For example, the string "C-compiler" really acts like the secret declaration ˜**string1**, where ˜**string1** has been predeclared by

static char ˜string1[ ] = "C-compiler";

The ~ implies that the name generated for the string is not specifiable by the programmer, so there can be no conflicts with string names secretly created by the compiler. See [2.4] for more on this.

1.5 Structure or union declarations

An external *structure declaration* is a data declaration with a type specifier of the flavor structure or union type, which is given by the syntax

```
structure-or-union-type  =
        [ struct |  union ] tag_opt
        parts-specification_opt

parts-specification  =
        {        { type-specifier
                 declarator-list ; }
        }
```

and a declarator that is a simple identifier. An example is

```
struct point { float x[2]; struct point *next; }
        first_point, last_point;
```

which declares **first_point** and **last_point** to be variables of a structured type identified by the tag **point**. The *parts-specification* enclosed in curly brackets defines a **struct point** to consist of an array of two floating values named x and a pointer to **struct point** named **next**. The variable **first_point** consists of two sub-variables that are denoted **first_point.x** and **first_point.next**. The *variable-name-expr* **first_point.x** names an array variable so **first_point.x[1]** names a **float** variable within the x part of the structured variable **first_point**. The complete story on *variable-name-exprs* must await Chapter 3.

The above declaration could have been written in the form

```
struct point {float x[2]; struct point *next;};
        struct point first_point, last_point;
```

The first line serves to define the content of the new type **struct point** but does not declare any names as variables of this type. The second line declares two variables of the new type. The structure tag **point** serves as an abbreviation for the content described, as well as allowing self-referential pointers within a structure. The *parts-specification* is only optional if the structure tag already has been defined by a *parts-specification* in an earlier declaration. The structure tag is optional only if a *parts-specification* is present.

When the keyword **union** is used instead of **struct**, the parts are made to overlay each other so that variables of such a union type at any point in time are holding a value corresponding to just one of the parts. For example,

```
union { double d; float f[2]; } u;
```

declares **u** to be a variable whose value is at any instant either double or an array of two floats. Sometimes, it is meaningful to say **u.d** and sometimes **u.f[1]**.

It is necessary to define some predicate, independent of the union, to determine its current contents. Unions can be safely used as part of a structure, one of whose parts is a small variable (**char** or **short int**), identifying which variant is actually present. Each value of the union type then is associated with a datum that tells which part names are appropriate to use. An example is

```
struct {
        char vtag;
        union {
                double d;
                float f[2];
                char str[4];
                }
        var;
        }
        u,v;
```

Now the program can test if **u.vtag** is **1**, say, before allowing any references to **u.var.d**, and similarly check **u.vtag** against **3** before using **u.var.str**. Note, however, that the language does not require such a tag variable to be associated with a union; any form of predicate is acceptable.

$$compound\text{-}statement.$$

where declarator must again be a scalar type, argument is a simple identifier, and

$$argument\text{-}declaration =$$
$$type\text{-}specifier\ declarator\text{-}list\ ;$$

Thus, the arguments to the function are specified as a comma-separated list of identifiers, enclosed in parentheses and possibly followed by a list of declarations that provide typing information for the arguments.

An argument must be of scalar type, or coercible to scalar (i.e., not a structure), and have names that are distinct from each other. The *argument-declaration-list* must contain declarations only for arguments in the immediately preceding *argument-list;* the arguments may be declared in any order, but may be declared once at most. An *argument-list* is optional, in which case there are no arguments.

The meaning of compound statement, and how to define a function body, will be discussed in [2.6].

The declaration

```
double sqrt (d)
    double d;
    {--------}
```

declares **sqrt** to be a function returning double when called with a single argument of type double. A more complicated example follows:

```
char * p (ac,c)
    char ac [ ];
    char c;
    { body }
```

which declares **p** to be a function returning a pointer to **char**, called with the name of an array of **chars** (corresponding to **ac**), and a **char** (corresponding to **c**).

Note that, for a variety of reasons, both of these argument declarations are misleading because of the way **c** evaluates expressions in general and actual parameters to function calls in particular. Thus, **ac** is actually a pointer to **char**, while **c** is most likely an **int**. These mysteries will be explored in [3.6].

1.7 Composite types

Up to this point, we have considered very simple forms of declarator, mostly identifiers standing alone or with some simple qualification. The full syntax rule for declarator is

$$
\begin{array}{ll}
declarator = & \\
\quad [\ identifier & \\
\quad |\ *declarator & \%\ pointer \\
\quad |\ declarator\ (\ ) & \%\ function \\
\quad |\ declarator\ [\ constant\text{-}expr_{opt}\ ] & \%\ array \\
\quad |\ (\ declarator\ ) & \%\ association\ control \\
\quad] &
\end{array}
$$

The form of this rule shows that a declarator is built from a unique identifier by a succession of qualifications (pointer to, function returning, or array of) and occasional parentheses to override the default associations in declarators. The syntax of a declarator matches the syntax of valid expressions involving the imbedded identifier; hence, the meaning of a compound declarator can be read from the inside out starting with the identifier, as can be seen from the examples given below.

The declaration

```
int *api[4], *fpi( );
```

makes **api** an array of pointer to integer and **fpi** a function returning values of type pointer to integer. The declaration

```
struct { int left, right; } *(*papst)[ ];
```

makes **papst** the name of a variable of type *pointer to array of pointers to structures consisting of integer parts left and right.* The parentheses are needed to force the identifier **papst** to associate more closely with the * rather than the preferred [ ]. The postfix array or function brackets bind more tightly than the prefix pointer symbol, so parentheses also are required in

```
int (*pai)[3], (*pfi)( );
```

to make a **pai** a pointer to array of integer and **pfi** a pointer to function returning integer.

(1) If τ is a *type-specifier* and *id* an *identifier,* then the declaration τ *id* ; makes *id* a variable of type τ.

(2) If D_{id} is a declarator with unique identifier *id* and τ D_{id} ; makes *id* a variable of type T_τ and D_x means declarator D_{id} with its unique *id* replaced by *x*, then

(a) τ $D_{(*id)}$; makes *id* a pointer to T_τ

(b) τ $D_{id[\ ]}$; makes *id* an array of T_τ

(c) τ $D_{id(\ )}$; makes *id* a function returning T_τ

(d) **typedef** τ D_{id} ; implies *id* equivalent to T_τ whenever *id* occurs as a type name.

The intent of these rules is to make the binding of declarations closely model how they are used in expressions (see Chapter 3). The operators [ ] (subscripted by) and ( ) (function called with arguments) bind from the identifier outward. Both type definition and parenthesizing call for deviations from this implied order of binding, and hence lead to conceptual difficulties. Type definitions offer the tremendous advantage, however, of permitting a complex type to be built a bit at a time.

A type definition has the syntax

type-definition =
        typedef *type-specifier declarator-list* ;

The type definition

    typedef float *pf_type ;

makes the name **pf_type** into a type name, which is an abbreviation for *pointer to float.* A subsequent declaration

    pf_type apf[5], *ppf;

makes **apf** an array of five pointers to float and **ppf** a pointer to pointer to float.

The following sequence of type definitions shows how very complex declarators like **papst** shown on the previous page can be avoided:

    typedef char FCH( ) ;   /* function returning char */
    typedef FCH *PFCH ;   /* pointer to FCH */
    typedef PFCH APFCH[ ] ;   /* array of PFCH */
    typedef APFCH *PAPFCH ;   /* pointer to APFCH */
    PAPFCH papfch ;   /* papfch is pointer to APFCH */

Using the established meaning for **PAPFCH**, we easily can declare a function returning values of this type by

    PAPFCH fpapfch( );

More useful examples of type definitions, structure and pointer declarations, and so on, are

    typedef struct {float real, imag; } COMPLEX;

    typedef COMPLEX CVECTOR[4];

    typedef CVECTOR CMATRIX[4];

    typedef CMATRIX *PCM;

    typedef PCM PCMFUNC( );

which finally define the type name **PCMFUNC** as meaning the class of functions returning a pointer to complex matrix, where the latter is a type consisting of an array of four vectors, which are arrays of four complex, which are structures with two floating parts. The type named **PCM** would have frequent usefulness as the argument and return type of functions manipulating these four by four complex matrices.

The following summarizes the external declaration syntax:

C-program =
    { *program-file* }

program-file =
    { [*function-declaration* | *type-definition*
    | *data-declaration*
    ]
    }

data-declaration =
    [**extern**$_{def}$| **static**]$_{opt}$
    type-specifier$_{opt}$ *initializable-declarator-list*$_{opt}$;

type-specifier =
    [*integer-type* | *floating-type*
    | *type-name* | *structure-or-union-type*]

initializable-declarator =
    declarator intializer$_{opt}$

integer-type =
    [**char** | [**unsigned** | **short** | **long**]$_{opt}$ **int**$_{def}$]

floating-type =
    [**short**$_{opt}$ **double** | **long**$_{opt}$ **float**]

structure-or-union-type =
    [**struct** | **union**] *tag*$_{opt}$
    parts-specification$_{opt}$

    % *parts-specification optional only if identifier*
    % *present and predeclared as struct-or-union tag*

parts-specification =
    { { *type-specifier declarator-list* ; } }
    % *no declarators allowed for functions*
    % *or arrays of indeterminate length*

declarator =
    [*identifier*
    | * *declarator*   % *pointer*
    | *declarator* ( )   % *function*
    | *declarator* [*constant-expr*$_{opt}$]   % *array*
    | (*declarator*)   % *association control*
    ]

type-definition =
    typedef *type-specifier declarator-list* ;

function-declaration =
  [function-definition | declarator ( )]

function-definition =
  [extern$_{def}$ | static]$_{opt}$
  type-specifier$_{opt}$ declarator (argument-list$_{opt}$)
  argument-declaration-list$_{opt}$
  compound-statement

argument-declaration =
  type-specifier declarator-list ;

2: INITIALIZERS

Beginnings are such perilous times.

— Frank Herbert, *Dune*

2.0 Introduction

Initializers are a convenient way to ensure that certain variables have meaningful values at the beginning of a program execution, or to construct tables of constants to aid run-time computation. Function declarations, which form the core of most C programs, also can be looked on as having initializers for objects of type function.

The syntax governing data initializers is

initializable-declarator =
   declarator initializer$_{opt}$

initializer =
   =$_{opt}$ *[expr | { initializer-list ,*$_{opt}$ *}]*

Note that a trailing comma is explicitly permitted, to simplify writing long lists. A very simple *initializable-declarator* is

double x −0.2E3;

while in the following declaration:

COMPLEX vector[3] =
   {{ 0, 1 }, {−3.14, 2.718}, {0.3, 4.1E−13}};

there is a complex initializer consisting of a list of three initializers, one for each element of the array of three **COMPLEX**. Each of the three initializers in the list is itself a list of initializers for the two parts of a **COMPLEX** structure. See [1.7] for the definition of the type named **COMPLEX**.

Any initializer occurring in an external declaration must be a constant expression, but this may include pointer expressions like

```
* &c[2].real
```

where c has been declared to be a **static** array of **COMPLEX**. The **&** operator delivers the location of the variable **c[2].real**, which can be computed at compile-time. This expression is of type pointer to float and might appear in the declaration

```
static float *fptr = &c[2].real;
```

Initializers in local declarations (see Chapter 4) must involve only expressions that can be calculated at entry to the compound statement housing the declarations. Externals may not be initialized in local declarations.

The constants in an initializer are effectively assigned to the corresponding variables, although not all coercions are performed that would be permitted in an assignment (see [3.1]). For example, in the above initializer for **vector**, the variables **vector[0].real** and **vector[0].imag** are initialized by the floating equivalents 0.0 and 1.0 for the integer constants 0 and 1, which are specified. Initializing an integer with a floating literal, on the other hand, is not generally supported.

An external name must not be initialized more than once, although multiple declarations are permitted and even necessary among program files in order to provide inter-program file communication.

Some implementations require that each external declaration be initialized exactly once, to fix the defining instance of the object; others require at least the use of the **extern** keyword with one declaration, while still others generally will accept the absence of any initializers. The safest practice appears to be to pick one instance of a multiply declared variable as the defining instance; give it the **extern** attribute explicitly, and give it an initializer, even if it is just **0**.

2.1 Integer initializers

An *integer initializer* has one of the simple forms

$=_{opt}$ { *expr* }

where *expr* is of type integer or character and is constant for a static or external initializer. For example,

static int number = 2 + 3, k = 'A'

causes **number** to have the initial value 5 and **k** the initial value of the result of lengthening the character constant **'A'** to integer type (see [3.1]).

If the value of the expression is too large to be properly represented, it is truncated on the left − with no warning. It generally is not permissible to use floating literals as integer initializers.

2.2 Floating initializers

A *floating initializer* has one of the forms

$=_{opt}$ { *expr* }

where *expr* is of type floating or else can be widened to floating. An initializer for a static or external declaration must evaluate to a constant, just as for integers; but the compiler will perform only integer arithmetic, so **2 × 3.142** is not allowed. The only operator permitted with floating literal initializers is unary minus.

Examples of valid floating intializers are

float x = 0.23−E5, y = 2 * 3, z = '0';

Note that **z** will be initialized to the floating representation of the integer that is the internal character code (machine-dependent) of character zero. If excessive precision is specified in a floating literal, or if the value cannot be properly represented in the target machine, the compiler will not, in general, complain.

2.3 Pointer initializers

A *pointer initializer* has one of the forms

$$=_{opt} \{ expr \}$$

where *expr* is an expression of type pointer and is calculable at compile-time in the case of a static or external declaration. In general, this means that the expression must reduce to an integer or to the address of a previously declared variable, plus or minus an integer. Some examples are

```
COMPLEX cvector[4];
float *fptr = &cvector[2].imag;
```

The expression **&cvector[2].imag** is an expression of type pointer to floating because **cvector[2].imag** is a *name-expr* denoting the **imag** part of the third element of array **cvector** and the **&** operator delivers the location of the named variable. Since **2** is a constant and **imag** is located at a fixed offset within **cvector[2]**, the pointer value is known at compile-time. The following pointer expressions also are allowed:

```
int k[5];
int *iptr = &k[1] + 2, *jptr = &k[4] − 1;
```

The expressions **&k[1]** and **&k[4]** are of type pointer to **int**, and **ptr** $\pm$ **int** is allowed as a pointer expression (see [3.3]) so these initializers are constant pointers to integer.

Whenever unsubscripted array names, string constants, structure names, union names, or function names without parameters appear, they are interpreted as pointers. Hence, the following also are valid initializers:

```
int (*pfi)( ) = distance;
char *pch = "what?";
float vector[10] , *fptr = vector;
```

The variable **pfi** is a pointer to function returning integer, initialized to point to **distance**; **pch** is pointer to character, initialized to point at the first character (subscript 0) of the constant string "what?"; **fptr** is pointer to float, initialized to point at **vector[0]**.

It is permissible to initialize a pointer to point at an undeclared identifier, but the practice is not recommended. Similarly, pointers may be initialized to integer values, but this practice is extremely machine-dependent for all values but zero and should be reserved for writing system code.

2.4 Array initializers

An *array initializer* has the form

$$=_{opt} expr \mid \{ \ initializer\text{-}list \ , \ _{opt} \}$$

where *expr* initializes only the first element, or where each initializer in *initializer-list* is a proper initializer for an element of the array. For example,

float x[4] = {0.0, 1.0, 3E−6, −1};

is correct because 0.0 is a floating constant and x[0] is a floating variable in array x, etc. When elements of the array are themselves arrays, the initializers must be bracketed *initializer-lists,* as in the following:

char page[3][5] =
    { "xxxx", {'y', '.', '.', 'y', '\0'}}

Here the string **"xxxx"** is shorthand for the *initializer-list* {'x', 'x', 'x', 'x', '\0'}. The first row of **page** (i.e., **page[0]**) is initialized to **"xxxx"**, the second row to **"y..y"** and the third row is initialized to zero (i.e., a row of '\0') by default since the outer *initializer-list* ends early. Note that a row size of **5** is needed for strings of size 4, to include the terminating '\0'.

The initializer

int matrix[3][3] = {{1}, {2,3}, {4}};

initializes **matrix[0][0]** to **1** as specified and the remainder of row 0 to **0** by default; **matrix[1][0]** is set to **2**, **matrix[1][1]** to **3**, and **matrix[1][2]** to **0**; finally, **matrix[2][0]** is set to **4** and the rest of the row to **0**.

Inside braces may be omitted, provided that all initializers are present and provided that all array sizes have been specified. The following initializer, although not recommended, has the same effect as the one above:

int matrix[3][3] = {1, 0, 0, 2, 3, 0, 4, 0, 0};

Furthermore, the size of the outer array may be implicitly given
by the size of an *initializer-list* as in

> **float vector[ ] = {0.1, 0.2, 0.3, 0.4};**

which is identical to the same declaration with **vector[4]**. Only
the left-most array size specification should be empty, as in

> **int matrix[ ][3] = {{1}, {2, 3}, {4}};**

which is once again equivalent to the above. Auto arrays may
not be initialized; separate scalar assignments must be made in
the function body.

2.5 Structure initializers

The *structure initializer*, like an array initializer, has the following form:

$$=_{opt} expr \mid \{ \ initializer\text{-}list \,_{,opt} \}$$

where the *expr* initializes only the first element or where each initializer of the list taken in order must be a valid initializer for
the corresponding part of the structure; parts are in the same
order as given by the structure declaration. For example,

> **struct node {int degree; char name[5];**
> **float weight; struct node *next;};**
>
> **struct node first_node =**
> **{2, "Node", 3.7E4, &other_node};**

These declarations make **first_node** a variable of type **struct node**
and initialize the parts, as follows:

first_node.degree	*is*	2
first_node.name	*is*	"Node" or {'N', 'o', 'd', 'e', '\0'}
first_node.weight	*is*	3.7E4
first_node.next	*points at*	other_node

A more complicated example is

> **struct {COMPLEX matrix[2][2]; char tag;}**
> **cmat =**
> **{/* first the matrix */**
> **{**
> **{{-1, 0}, {0, 1}}, /* row 0 */**
> **{{-3.2, 5.}}, /* row 1 */**
> **},**
> **/* then the tag */**
> **'M'**
> **},**

Here **cmat** has been declared as a variable of type structure with parts **matrix** and **tag**. Hence, its initializer has the general form

> { *initializer-for-matrix* , *char-constant* }

Since matrix is of type array of **COMPLEX**, its initializer has the form

> { *initializer-for-row-0* ,
> *initializer-for-row-1*
> }

and so on. Finally, each initializer for a **COMPLEX** structure has the form

> { *initializer-for-real-part* , *initializer-for-imag-part* }

and so the complete initializer for **cmat** emerges from a sequence of stepwise refinements. Note that the first element of the first row of **cmat.matrix** has not been explicitly initialized. In the case of external declarations, it would be {**0.0, 0.0**} by default.

If an initializer is specified for a union, it must correspond to the *first* of the declared parts. Neither unions nor structures may be initialized in automatic declarations.

2.6 Function definitions

A *function definition* looks somewhat like a data declaration that is initialized − therefore, its discussion in this section. Indeed, the arguments and function body constitute the value associated with a function name, so they do play a role similar to initializer, except that function names represent constant (unchangeable) values, not variables. Variables of type pointer to function may change their allegiance but functions may not!

The syntax of a function definition is

$$function\text{-}definition \ =$$
$$[\ \textbf{extern}_{def}|\ \textbf{static}\ ]_{opt}$$
$$type\text{-}specifier_{opt}\ declarator\ (\ argument\text{-}list_{opt}\ )$$
$$argument\text{-}declaration\text{-}list_{opt}$$
$$compound\text{-}statement$$

The simplest form of compound statement is a brace-enclosed sequence of statements (imperative commands). Here is a complete function definition:

```
double length(x,y;)
    double x,y;
    {
    return sqrt(x * x + y * y);
    }
```

The names x and y are formal arguments for the function **length** and they behave like special variables, which are initialized to different values each time the function is called. It, therefore, is not permissible to have explicit initializers in an argument specification. An appearance of **length(0.0, p[2])** is equivalent to

sqrt(0.0 * 0.0 + p[2] * p[2])

Complex function declarators like **(*fpa( ))[ ]** can be avoided via type definitions as presented in [1.7], so their explanation will be postponed until Chapter 4.

Before examining compound statement in detail, it is instructive to distinguish pointer arguments from other arguments. The only way that a function can alter the value of some variable x in the environment from which the function is called is to be passed the location **&x** of x, where the corresponding formal argument is of pointer type. Also, aggregate types (struct, union, or array) cannot be passed as arguments directly, but pointers to them may. The function shown on the following page is intended to replace **index** by the first subscript position where value x is equal to an element of array **table**:

```
float table[6] = {0, 0, 1, 2, 3, 7}, x = 2;
int index;
main( )
      {
      lookup(&table[0], x, &index);
      }

lookup(t, val, i)
      float *t, val;
      int *i;
      {
      int k;
      for (k = 0; k < 6; ++k)
            if (*(t + k) == val)
                  {
                  *i = k;
                  return;
                  }
      *i = -1;
      }
```

Some of this will not be clear until pointer expressions and *variable-name-exprs* are fully understood; see in particular [3.1] and [3.3]. It is important to realize that following **&index**, the actual argument corresponding to the formal pointer argument **i**, is made; then, assignments like *i = k; actually mean assignments to **index**, because the prefix pointer operation * makes the expression *i a valid *name-expr* for an alterable object in the memory.

The above program can be rewritten changing **&table[0]** to **table**, **float *t** to **float t[ ]** and ***(t + k)** to **t[k]** with no alteration of meaning. This is because unsubscripted array names are taken to mean the value of a pointer to the 0-th element, because formal array arguments are interpreted as pointers to the array element type, and because **t[k]** is implemented as the expression ***(t + k)** anyway (see [3.4]).

It is finally time to describe some statements. The basic unit of function definition is compound statement, whose syntax is presented as follows:

compound-statement =
    { { [*local-declaration* | *type-definition*] }_opt
    { *statement* }_opt }

The detailed discussion of these local declarations and type definitions, which are largely the same as the external declarations, is in Chapter 4. For now, we will concentrate on the statements, or imperative commands, of the C language.

The formal syntax rule for *statement* is

```
statement =
    [ expr ;                      % assignments and function calls
    | compound-statement         % for grouping
    | selection-statement
    | repetition-statement
    | interruption-statement
    | labeled-statement
    | ;                          % null statement
    ]
```

Although detailed discussion of expressions (i.e., *exprs*) must await Chapter 3, we will introduce simple assignment expressions (statements in most languages) and function calls (procedure or subroutine calls elsewhere), since they are the active workhorses of most C programs. Some expression statements already encountered are

```
k = 0;
++k; /* same as k = k + 1; */
lookup(table, x, &index);
```

Programs unable to make choices are weak indeed, so C has two flavors of selection statement:

```
selection-statement =
    [ if ( logical-expr ) statement
        ( else statement )
                            opt
    | switch ( expr ) switch-statement-group ]

switch-statement-group =
    { {[ local-declaration | type-definition ]}
        { case-prefixed-statement } }
                                        opt

case-prefixed-statement =
    { [ case constant-expr | default ] : } statement
```

An **if** statement calls for execution of the first substatement precisely when the *logical-expr* is "true" (nonzero); otherwise, it calls for the execution of the second substatement after **else**.

When the **else** phrase is omitted, it is just as if **else /* null */;** were explicitly specified. For example,

```
if (k < 2)
        p = f(k);
else
        p = g(2 - k);
```

will perform exactly one of the two assignments depending on the magnitude of **k** relative to **2**. Relational operators deliver a value of 1 for "true" and 0 for "false" as is more fully discussed in Chapter 3. A common form is

```
if (p)
    . . .
else if (q)
    . . .
else if (r)
    . . .
else    /* none of the above */
    . . .
```

and this style of indentation is recommended.

Frequently enough, the *logical-exprs* **p**, **q**, **r**, and so forth, are of the form **k==1**, **k==2**, **k==5**, etc., where **==** is the equality comparison operator in C. Such cases are catered for by the **switch** statement as exemplified by

```
switch(k - 2)
        {
        case 3: j = k*k; break;
        case 5, 2: ++k; do_something(k); break;
        default: error ("bad k");
        }
```

Since the **case** prefix allows only constant expressions, the **switch** statement can be implemented very efficiently. The **break** statements are necessary to terminate the **switch** statement after each selectable portion; otherwise, control flows from one **case** to the next in a most unsatisfactory manner. **Case** labels may occur embedded within a compound statement. Only an embedded **switch** statement limits this questionable facility.

The repetition statements of C are given by

```
repetition-statement =
    [ while ( logical-expr ) statement
    | do statement while ( logical-expr );
    | for ( expr_opt ; logical-expr_opt ; expr_opt ) statement
    ]
```

A **while** statement repeatedly performs its substatement until the *logical-expr* is no longer "true," never embarking on an execution of the substatement if *logical-expr* is "false." It may be a repetition of multiplicity 0 if *logical-expr* is initially "false."

The **do** statement is similar except that the test is performed and the repetition potentially terminated *after* each performance of the substatement. It therefore performs its substatement at least once.

The **for** statement is a shorthand for

```
expr_1;
while ( logical-expr_2 )
        { statement ; expr_3;}
```

so the first expression is usually an initialization; the second a logical pretest; and the third some form of post-augmentation. Examples are

```
while (c[i] == ' ' && i < SIZE)
        ++i;
do      {
        swap (c, i, j);
        ++i;
        --j;
        }
        while (i < j);
/* array c now reversed */
for (i = 0; i < SIZE; ++i)
        {
        a[i] = b[i];
        c[i] = -1.0;
        }
/* array b copied to a and c set to -1.0 */
```

If the *logical-expr* in a **for** statement is missing, a constant "true" value (1) is assumed.

It occasionally is convenient to interrupt the normal sequence of statements by one of the following:

>*interruption-statement* =
>   [**break** ;
> | **continue** ;
> | **return** *expr*$_{opt}$;
> | **goto** *identifier* ;
>   ]

The **break** statement causes termination of the smallest enclosing repetition or **switch** statement.

The **continue** statement causes termination of the repeatable substatement of the smallest enclosing repetition statement. Execution resumes with the augmentation part of a **for** or with the test part of a **do** or **while**.

A **return** statement terminates execution of the enclosing function. If an *expr* is specified, it becomes the returned value of the function after conversion to the declared type of the function; if there is no expression, the value returned by the function is garbage. At the end of every function body, there is an implicit **return** with no expression.

A **goto** statement specifies that execution should resume at the statement labeled by the identifier. Finally, a labeled statement has the syntax

>*labeled-statement* =
>   *identifier* : *statement*

and serves as a target for **goto** statements. Only one such definition of a given label may occur within the same function. Since labeled statement is a legal form of statement, it follows that any number of labels may occur in sequence. In practice, **break** is needed rarely, **continue** never, and **goto** even less often than that. It follows that labels need never be used if **goto** is avoided. It also is good style to minimize the number of **return** statements; exactly one at the end of the function is best of all for readability.

2.7 Initializer syntax

All data initializers take the form

initializer =
$=_{opt}$ [*expr* | { *initializer-list* $,_{opt}$ }]

and all function initializers are compound statements of the form

compound-statement =
{ { [*local-declaration* | *type-definition*] }$_{opt}$
{ *statement* }$_{opt}$ }

statement =
[*expr* ;   % *assignments and function calls*
| *compound-statement*   % *for grouping*
| *selection-statement*
| *repetition-statement*
| *interruption-statement*
| *labeled-statement*
| ;   % *null statement*
]

selection-statement =
[**if** (*logical-expr*) *statement*
(**else** *statement*)$_{opt}$
| **switch** (*expr*) *switch-statement-group*
]

switch-statement-group =
{ { [*local-declaration* | *type-definition*] }$_{opt}$
{ *case-prefixed-statement* } }

case-prefixed-statement =
{ [**case** *constant-expr* | **default**] : } *statement*

repetition-statement =
[**while** (*logical-expr*) *statement*
| **do** *statement* **while** (*logical-expr*) ;
| **for** (*expr*$_{opt}$; *logical-expr*$_{opt}$; *expr*$_{opt}$) *statement*
]

interruption-statement =
[**break** ;
| **continue** ;
| **return** *expr*$_{opt}$;
| **goto** *identifier* ;
]

labeled-statement =
identifier : *statement*

3: EXPRESSIONS

The result we proceed to divide, as you see,
By Nine Hundred and Ninety and Two:
Then subtract Seventeen, and the answer must be
Exactly and perfectly true.

— Lewis Carroll, *Hunting of the Snark*

3.0 Introduction

The expressions of C actually carry out the work (change of state of variables) of the program. In particular, a simple assignment replaces the current value of some variable by a newly calculated value and has the syntax

variable-name-expr = *expr*

The *variable-name-exprs* range in degree of complexity from simple identifiers of integer variables to complicated name expressions like

pcm —> **matrix**[1][k].**imag**

which identifies the **imag** part of the complex member at row **1** and column **k** of the **matrix** part of the structure pointed at by pointer variable **pcm**. The remainder of this chapter will explain such expressions.

The expressions themselves are a wider class allowing many different operators to be combined with *variable-name-exprs* and constants and so provide the computational power of the language. These expressions range in complexity from simple integer constants up to things like

$$(m[k+2] >>3) \mid (p \rightarrow f * (*pfunc)(2,j))$$

which defies simple verbal description.

Before embarking on our extended voyage through operator-space, there are several topics of general interest that should be discussed at least briefly. The first is precedence and association of operators.

Whenever the sequence

$operand_1$ $binop_1$ $operand_2$ $binop_2$ $operand_3$

occurs (e.g., **a + b * c**), there is a potential ambiguity in the interpretation of the expression [e.g., **(a + b) * c** or **a + (b * c)**]. Each operator in C has a precedence-level, relative to other operators, which determines the association unambiguously if the two operators are at different levels. Since the multiply operator * has a higher level than the add operator **+**, the expression **a + b * c** means **a + (b * c)**. By use of parentheses the programmer can override these rules [e.g., by writing **(a + b) * c**].

Within the same precedence-level, most binary operators will associate "left to right." For example,

a + b − c + d *means* **((a + b) − c) + d**

The assignment operator, however, does just the opposite:

x = a[2] = j = 0 *means* **x = (a[2] = (j = 0))**

The unary operators are all at the same level and higher than all binary operators. They associate from right to left as one would expect since they are mostly in prefix position. For example,

−*pi

means the negative of the integer pointed to by **pi**. In most cases, the language does not prescribe the order of evaluation of subexpressions, so that **a * b + c * d** may be calculated by doing **(a * b)** first, then **(c * d)**, or vice versa. This has definite significance for expressions like

(t = f(a)) + g(t)

whose value is not guaranteed to be computed reproducibly. The programmer is warned to be careful in the use of assignment expressions within calculations. The language also allows the implementation to rearrange expressions with like commutative operators:

$$\mathbf{a + b + c} \text{ is } \mathbf{(a + c) + b} \text{ or } \mathbf{(a + b) + c}, \text{ etc.}$$

The arithmetic types (integer and floating) fall into a natural hierarchy from **char** to **double**, which is called the widening hierarchy:

$$\mathbf{char} \rightarrow \mathbf{short} \rightarrow \mathbf{int} \rightarrow \mathbf{unsigned} \rightarrow \mathbf{long} \rightarrow \mathbf{float} \rightarrow \mathbf{double}$$

which determines the type of value returned by many of the operators when the two operands have different arithmetic type. For example, in

$$\mathbf{(i + '0') - x} \quad /* \text{ i is int, x float } */$$

the **char** value **'0'** is widened to integer which then can be added to **i**; then this integer result is widened to floating so that the floating **x** can be subtracted to produce a final floating result. The language also has *cast* operators, which explicitly request such widenings, so the above is equivalent to

$$\mathbf{(float)(i + (int)'0') - x}$$

The normal rule for binary arithmetic operators calls for widening the narrower operand to the wider one. The language reserves the right to perform arithmetic by widening operands more than necessary just to satisfy this rule. Thus, **char** and **short** operands are frequently widened to **int,** while **float** arithmetic often is performed in **double.** The distinction usually is not highly visible to the programmer.

When the type of a *variable-name-expr* is wider than the type of the expression assigned to it, the normal widening will occur; when it is narrower, the conversion is machine-dependent and prone to information-loss, so that narrowing assignments should be used sparingly.

C programs may contain *conditional-exprs* whose syntax is

conditional-expr =
   logical-expr ? *expr* : *expr*

They are used to avoid repeating most of an expression in an **if else** when only part depends on some condition. For example,

$$x = (y < 3.0) ? -1.0 : 1 ;$$

assigns to **x** the value **−1.0** if **y** is less than **3.0**; otherwise, the value **1.0** is assigned. The rules of the language stipulate that one or the other but not both *exprs* are evaluated. The result is always the wider of the types of the two *exprs* so that the integer **1** above is widened to **1.0** before assignment to **x**.

Full assignment possibilities are given by the syntax rule

```
assignment-expr =
    [ variable-name-expr binop_opt = expr
    | [ ++ | −− ] scalar-variable-name-expr
    | scalar-variable-name-expr [ ++ | −− ] ]
            % scalar means arithmetic or pointer

binop =
    [ + | − | * | / | %
    | & | | | ^ | << | >> ]
```

Assignments like **x += y** replace **x** by the value of **x + y**, but **x** is not calculated twice. To double **x[i, j]**, one simply can write

```
x[i, j] *=2
```

Assignments like **++x**, **−−x** are equivalent respectively to **(x += 1)**, **(x −= 1)**. All *assignment-exprs* return a value that is the value of the variable before or after the assignment takes place. Of the three forms of *assignment-expr,* only the postfix augmentation operators **(++, −−)** deliver the value before assignment. For example,

```
k = 0;              /* k is 0 */
n = k++;            /* n is 0, k is 1 */
m = (k *= 2);       /* m and k are 2 */
k = −−n;            /* k and n are −1 */
n += (n++) − n      /* ouch! no promises */
```

It should be kept in mind that the language does *not* specify an order of evaluation of the two operands of an assignment, so that

```
i = 2;
a[i] = x + (i = 3)     /* a[i] is a[2] or a[3] ? */
```

is not deterministic.

The C language has sequence expressions that consist of a sequence of expressions separated by commas, that is, an *expr-list*. It is recommended to package a *sequence-expr* in enclosing parentheses since sometimes they may occur in a context in which commas have other meanings as well, as in an argument list. The meaning of

$$(t = x, s = y - f(t), s*7.3)$$

is much the same as if we wrote the compound statement

$$\{t = x, s = y - f(t); s*7.3\}$$

in the place of an expression. The three subexpressions are evaluated in order from left to right as would be implied by the semicolons in the analogous compound statement; the value delivered is the value of the last (right-most) *expr* of the list.

3.1 Integer expressions

The basic *integer expressions* are the so-called integer primaries, which include integer constants, integer and character variable names, integer function calls (see [3.6]), and parenthesized integer expressions. The following are integer primaries:

$$25 \quad k \quad count(p,3) \quad (i - 2 * k)$$

More complicated name expressions like

$$p -> q[k].n$$

will be treated in subsequent sections.

Integer primaries can be combined with other integer expressions using the unary operators $+$ and $-$, or one of the binary operators $+$, $-$, $*$, $/$, $\%$. The integer quotient ($/$) and remainder ($\%$) operators produce the expected quotient and remainder (truncated toward zero) when both operands are positive. The result is otherwise somewhat machine-dependent. The other three operators are those of normal integer arithmetic. For example, $3+6$ is 9, $3-5$ is -2, $3*12$ is 36, $17/5$ is 3 and $17\%5$ is 2.

The following is an integer arithmetic expression:

$$25 + k \% \text{count}(p,3) - 7 / (i - 2 * k)$$

It also is possible to combine integer expressions using bitwise binary operators **&**, **|**, **^**, **<<**, **>>**, and the unary bitwise operator **~**. They are known respectively as "and," "or," "exclusive or," "left shift," "right shift," and "complement." "Complement" considers its operand as a sequence of binary digits and flips the state of each such "bit." The "and," "or," and "exclusive or" consider both operands as sequences of binary digits and perform the well-known bitwise operations. The shifts consider the first operand as a sequence of binary digits to be left- or right-shifted the number of bit positions given by the second operand, which should be positive for maximum portability. Left shifts introduce zero bits from the right, but right shifts in general are not promised to do so for negative values of the first operand. For example,

(000101) & (010110)	*is*	(000100)
(000111) | (110100)	*is*	(110111)
(000111) ^ (110100)	*is*	(110011)
(000101) << 2	*is*	(010100)
(001100) >> 3	*is*	(000001)
~(001100)	*is*	(110011)

The following statement extracts the low-order eight-bit byte from **k** and inserts it into the high-order eight-bit byte of **p**, assuming 16-bit integer variables:

$$p = (p\&0377) \mid (k\&0xFF) << 8$$

The expression **p&0377** saves the low byte of **p** and has a zero-high byte. The expression **(k&0xFF)** <<8 has as high byte the low byte of **k** and a zero-low byte. Hence, the bitwise "or" has a high byte equal to the low byte of **k** and a low byte equal to the low byte of **p**. The following two expressions are also the same (on a 16-bit computer):

$$p \text{ ^ } 0xFFFF \quad is \quad \text{~}p$$

An integer expression also results from taking the difference of two *pointer-exprs* to the same type. For example, if **a** is an array of **int**, then

&a[3] − &a[1]

is the difference between two pointers divided by the size of **int**. Hence, the value is 2. If the two pointers do not point into the same array, bizarre results may occur. See [3.3] for details of *pointer-exprs.*

There also are integer constants of the form

sizeof *[expr |* (*type-expr*) *]*

which deliver the size in bytes of the operand *expr* or of the type designated by the cast (*type-expr*). The function **sizeof** applied to an *array-variable-name* or string yields the size of the entire array, as one would expect.

Finally, among the integer expressions are to be found the very important *logical-exprs,* whose syntax is

```
logical-expr =
    [ logical-expr && logical-expr
    | logical-expr || logical-expr
    | ! logical-expr
    | expr [ == | != ] expr
    | expr [ < | > | <= | >= ] expr
    | expr          % interpreted as (expr != 0)
    | ( logical-expr )
    ]
```

The logical AND **&&**, logical OR **||**, and logical NOT **!** operators are defined as equivalent to certain *conditional-exprs,* as follows:

a && b	≡	**a ? (b ? 1 : 0) : 0**
a || b	≡	**a ? 1 : (b ? 1 : 0)**
! a	≡	**a ? 0 : 1**

The result of these operators is always 0 or 1; therefore, an integer variable holding values generated by these operators can act as a boolean or logical variable. This is so because an integer expression encountered in the context of a test is interpreted as "true" when nonzero, and "false" otherwise. Notice that the **&&** and **||** determine an order of evaluation inherited from the meaning of the *conditional-expr.* Basically, they guarantee left to right evaluation with termination occurring as soon as the value is determined.

The equality operators (equal $==$ and not equal $!=$) as well as relational operators (less $<$, greater $>$, less or equal $<=$, greater or equal $>=$) yield 1 if the inequality is "true," and 0 otherwise. If one operand is narrower than the other, it is widened appropriately before the comparison.

A cast expression of the form

> **(int)** *arithmetic-expr*

gives the same integer value as would be obtained by assigning the *arithmetic-expr* to an **int** variable.

3.2 Floating expressions

The basic *floating expressions* are the floating primaries, which include floating constants, floating variable names, floating function calls, and parenthesized floating expressions, like

> **3.14159E−5   x[k − 1]   length(x, y)   (2.0 * z + y)**

More complicated floating expressions are built from floating primaries and from other floating expressions by the unary operators $+$ and $-$ and by the familiar binary arithmetic operators $+$, $-$, *, and /. For example,

> **3.14 * (x[k − 1] − length(x, y)) + z/1.1**

The augmentation operators $++$ and $--$ call for adding 1.0 or -1.0 to the floating variable specified. As with integers, both prefix and postfix forms apply. The precision of a floating calculation will be at least as precise as the wider (more precise) of the two operands. Some implementations may use extra precision during the calculation.

A cast expression of the form

> **(float)** *arithmetic-expr*

widens the *arithmetic-expr* to **float**, if necessary.

Integers may be intermixed freely with floating operands, and are widened as needed.

3.3 Pointer expressions

There are no pointer constants, strictly speaking, so the primaries of type pointer are *pointer variable names, pointer function calls,* and *parenthesized pointer expressions.* The basic pointer expression is of the form

&*variable-name-expr*

examples of which are

&k   &c[2].f   &(p —> name)

the first two of which are constant pointer expressions if **k** and **c** are **static** or **extern** variables.

The only other *pointer-exprs* are of the form

pointer-expr [+ | −] integer-expr

which has a value given by the current address value of the *pointer-expr* plus or minus the *integer-expr* value scaled by the size of the type to which the pointer points. For example, if **a** is an array of **int** and if **ints** are of size 2, then **&a[0]+2** will be 4 more than the machine address at the beginning of array **a**. Hence, **&a[0]+2** ≡ **&a[2]**, which is the motivation for such a definition of pointer arithmetic.

The augmentation assignments (**++** and **−−**) can be applied to pointer variable names, in which case the above meaning of plus and minus are in effect. For example,

```
p = &a[0]; ++p;   /* p points at a[1] */
p += 2; −−p;      /* now at a[2] */
```

If an integer is assigned to a pointer variable, however, no scaling is performed. This is a hole left intentionally in the language type-checking to facilitate systems programming. Pointer expressions figure in other types of expressions because of the "dereferencing" operator * which, as a prefix to a *pointer-expr*, delivers the name of the variable pointed at by the value of the *pointer-expr*.

One of the more important uses of pointers in C is to efficiently walk through an array using the pointer augmentation assignments. The following will search an array of **chars** for the first **x**.

```
p = &str[0];
while (*p != 'x')
    ++p;
/* now p points at first str[k] == x */
```

3.4 Expressions involving arrays

The complex *variable-name-exprs* that C allows are built up from the dereferencing operator * applied to *pointer-exprs* (see [3.3]), the parts focussing operators . and −> applied to structures and structure pointers (see [3.5]), and the array element focussing expressions to be discussed in this section. An expression of the form

array-variable-name-expr [*integer-expr-list*]

denotes the element variable selected by the value of the *integer-expr-list*. As in the case of array declarations, **a[5, j, x+3]** is entirely equivalent to **a[5][j][x+3]**. Each value should clearly be nonnegative and less than the corresponding declared maximum number of elements in the array. For example,

```
int a[5], k;
k = 3;
a[4] = a[k] + a[k+1];    /* okay */
a[k+2] = 9           /* no good, a[4] is last */
```

A declaration with more than one dimension like

```
float x[5][3][2];
```

declares x to be a variable of type array of array of array of **float** so that **x[3]** is a legal *array-variable-name-expr* in its own right as is **x[3][2]**. Finally, **x[3][2][0]** is a *float-variable-name-expr* and may be used in calculations or may be assigned a new value.

Although usually not of interest to the programmer, the subscript notation obeys the equivalence

```
a[e] ≡ *((a) + (e))
```

where the array name **a** without subscript is taken to be equivalent to **&a[0]**, a pointer to the first element of **a**, and the **+** indicates pointer arithmetic.

Array names and strings are changed to *pointer-exprs* pointing at the first element whenever they appear as *exprs* unsubscripted and not as array initializers. For example, the following function call

> **printf("Here is a string %s", ch_array);**

passes two pointer arguments: the first, a pointer to **char** that points at 'H'; and the second, a pointer to the first element of the presumably **char** array **ch_array**.

3.5 Structure and union expressions

An expression of the form

> *structure-or-union-variable-name-expr . part-name*

denotes the subvariable (identified by *part-name*) within the specified *structure-or-union-variable*. Similarly, an expression of the form

> *structure-or-union-pointer-expr —> part-name*

denotes a part variable within the *structure-or-union* pointed at by the current value of the *pointer-expr*. For example,

```
struct point {float x[2]; struct point *next;}
        first_point, last_point, *top;
top = &first_point;
first_point.x[0] = 3.2;  /* same as top —> x[0] = 3.2; */
first_point.next = &last_point;
first_point.next —> x[0] = -1.0;
last_point.next = 0;  /* null pointer */
top —> x[1] = 3.9;
top —> x[0] = first_point.x[0];  /* changes nothing */
```

makes the pointer **top** point at the structure **first_point**, then the 0-th element of part **x** of **first_point** is changed to **3.2**, the **next** part of **first_point** is made to point at **last_point**, the 0-th element of part **x** of structure pointed at by **next** part of **first_point** is set to **-1.0**, the **next** part of **last_point** is made to point nowhere, and the 1-st element of part **x** of the structure pointed at by **top** is set to **3.9**. The final assignment does nothing but waste time since **top** points at **first_point**.

Structure and union references are not changed to pointers, as are array and function references, when they appear where a scalar is required in an expression. Hence, about all that you can do with a structure or union is select one of its parts or take its address. The following example shows how to use unions in a safe way:

```
struct card_variant {char vtag; char rank, suit;};
struct joker_variant {char vtag; int num;};
union {struct card_variant card;
       struct joker_variant joker;} deck[54];
/* initialize the deck of 52 cards & 2 jokers */
if (deck[k].card.vtag == 'C')
       {if (deck[k].card.suit == 'H') ...etc.}
else if (deck[k].card.vtag == 'J')
       {if (deck[k].joker.num < 3) ...etc.}
else
       {error ("bad card");}
```

3.6 Function calls

The functions of C are invoked by *function calls* of the following form:

function-name-expr (*expr-list*$_{opt}$)

where *function-name-expr* has the syntax rule

```
function-name-expr =
    [ function-name
    | (* function-pointer-expr )
    ]
```

The *function-name-exprs* range in complexity from simple names like **sqrt** to complicated ones like

(*p -> c[k - 2].pfch)

which means the function pointed to by the pointer part **pfch** of the $(k - 2)$-th item in array part **c** of the structure pointed to by pointer variable **p**. The parts focussing operators -> and . have the highest precedence (along with [ ] and ( )), so the dereferencing operator * is the last one applied in the above expression. See [3.7] for the complete story on operator precedence and association.

It is permissible for the *function-name-expr* to be an undeclared identifier, in which case it is taken as an external function returning integer. A function defined with no return statements (called a "void" function) should never be used as an *expr* where its value returned would matter; in other words, it only should appear as an expression statement, as any but the last *expr* in a *sequence-expr*, or as any but the test part of a **for**.

The *exprs* in the parenthesized list following the *function-name-expr* are called the *actual arguments* of the function call and they should correspond in number and type to the list of formal arguments specified in the function definition. For example, if **lookup** is declared (see [2.6]) as a function with the argument specifications

    (float *t, val; int *i;)

then each call to **lookup** should be of the form

    lookup(e_1, e_2, e_3)

where the e_k are *exprs,* respectively, of types pointer to floating, floating, and pointer to integer. In the absence of any argument declarations, as for an undeclared *function-name-expr*, or for a function declared with no arguments, or for arguments beyond those declared in the argument list, certain default coercions are applied. The functions **char** and **short** are widened to **int**, and **floats** are widened to **double**. If the function expects to receive **chars**, **shorts**, or **floats**, it is mandatory that the argument declarations be known to the calling function. It is permissible for an implementation to widen arguments as it sees fit, so long as both caller and callee know what to expect.

As an actual argument, an *array-variable-name-expr* or string that is not subscripted is interpreted as a pointer value to the first element of the array; a *function-name-expr* lacking the parenthesized list of arguments is similarly taken as a pointer value to the named function.

In a function definition, a formal array argument is interpreted to mean a pointer to the element type of the array; hence, all array arguments are essentially variable arguments in the sense that assignments, within a function definition, of the form **a[k] = e;** have the effect of changing the value of the **k**-th element in the array, which appears as the actual argument corresponding to the formal argument **a**. For example,

```
clear_array (float a[ ]; int n;)
        {
        int i;
        for (i=0; i<n; ++i)
                a[i] = 0.0;
        }
float x[5][5];
main( )
        {
        clear_array (x[2], 5); /* clear 2th row */
        }
```

causes the row **x[2]** of matrix **x[5][5]** to be cleared to floating zeros. The *expr* **x[2]** is a valid *array-variable-name-expr* with 5 elements of type **float**, which matches to formal argument **a** of type array of **float**. Each assignment **a[i] = 0.0;** in **clear_array** actually means **x[2][i] = 0.0;** during the execution of **clear_array** invoked by the call **clear_array (x[2], 5);**.

All functions in C may call themselves recursively, or call other functions that call them in turn. As an example of recursion, the following function returns the sum of the first **n** integers:

```
int sum (int n;)
{return (n <= 1 ? 1 : n + sum(n - 1));}
```

3.7 Expression syntax

The following summarizes the syntax of expressions in C:

```
expr =
        [ conditional-expr | assignment-expr
        | sequence-expr | arithmetic-expr
        | pointer-expr | cast-expr ]
```

```
arithmetic-expr =
        [ integer-expr |  floating-expr ]

integer-expr =
        [ integer-arithmetic-expr
        | bitwise-expr
        | logical-expr
        | pointer-difference
        | object-size-value
        | integer-cast-expr
        | integer-primary
        ]

integer-arithmetic-expr =
        [ [ + | − ] integer-expr
        | integer-expr [ + | − | * | / | % ] integer-expr
        ]

bitwise-expr =
        [ ~ integer-expr
        | integer-expr [ & | | | ^ | << | >> ]
                integer-expr
        ]

pointer-difference =
        pointer-expr − pointer-expr

object-size-value =
        sizeof [ expr | ( type-expr ) ]

logical-expr =
        [ logical-expr && logical-expr
        | logical-expr || logical-expr
        | ! logical-expr
        | expr [ == | != ] expr
        | expr [ < | > | <= | >= ] expr
        | expr            % interpreted as (expr != 0)
        | ( logical-expr )
        ]

integer-cast-expr =
        ( [ char | [ short | unsigned | long ] opt int ] ) arithmetic-expr

floating-expr =
        [ floating-expr [ + | − | * | / ] floating-expr
        | [ + | − ] floating-expr
        | floating-cast-expr
        | floating-primary ]
```

floating-cast-expr =
    [(**long**$_{opt}$ **float**) | (**short**$_{opt}$ **double**) *]* *floating-expr*

conditional-expr =
    logical-expr **?** *expr* **:** *expr*

assignment-expr =
    [variable-name-expr binop$_{opt}$ **=** *expr*
    | *[* **++** | **−−** *] scalar-variable-name-expr*
    | *scalar-variable-name-expr [* **++** | **−−** *]*
    ]   % *scalar means arithmetic or pointer*

binop =
    [**+** | **−** | ***** | **/** | **%**
    | **&** | **||** | **^** | **<<** | **>>**
    ]

sequence-expr =
    expr { **,** *expr* }

pointer-expr =
    [pointer-primary
    | **&***variable-name-expr*   % *but not array name*
    | *pointer-expr [* **+** | **−** *] integer-expr*
    ]

cast-expr =
    (*type-expr*) *expr*

type-expr =
    type-specifier abstract-declarator

abstract-declarator =
    [empty | ******abstract-declarator*
    | *abstract-declarator* ( )
    | *abstract-declarator* **[** *constant-expr*$_{opt}$ **]**
    | (*non-empty-abstract-declarator*)
    ]   % *a declarator with its identifier deleted*

primary =
    [constant | *variable-name-expr* | *string*
    | *function-name-expr* (*expr-list*$_{opt}$)
    | (*expr*)
    ]

function-name-expr =
    [function-name | ******pointer-expr*
    | *structure-or-union-variable-name-expr* **.** *part-name*
    | *structure-or-union-pointer-expr* **−>***part-name*
    | *array-variable-name-expr* **[** *expr* **]**
    ]

Operator Precedence and Association

Classes	Operators	Association
primary	. -> (*args*) [*subscript*]	→
unary	* & + - ! ~ ++ -- (*cast*) sizeof	←
mults	* / %	→
adds	+ -	→
shifts	<< >>	→
relational	< > <= >=	→
equality	== !=	→
bitwise and	&	→
bitwise xor	^	→
bitwise or	|	→
logical and	&&	→
logical or	||	→
conditional	$e_1 ? e_2 : e_3$	
assignment	= *binop*=	←
sequence	e_1, e_2	→

(Precedence level — brace spanning from primary to sequence)

The operators that allow rearrangement are

Commutative Binary Operators

    * + == != & ^ |

The following operators imply a fixed order of evaluation:

Forced Evaluation Order Operators

    && || $e_1 ? e_2 : e_3$ e_1, e_2

4: LOCAL DECLARATIONS

If anyone anything lacks
He'll find it all ready in stacks.

— W.S. Gilbert, *The Sorcerer*

4.0 Introduction

Each compound statement in a C program may begin with a sequence of local declarations or type definitions that serve to introduce names of objects or types whose declared properties are not known or relevant outside the enclosing compound statement. The local type definitions have the same syntax as the external ones, whereas the local declarations have the syntax

$$local\text{-}declaration =$$
$$[\ \textbf{auto}_{def}|\ \textbf{static}\ |\ \textbf{extern}\ |\ \textbf{register}\ ]_{opt}$$
$$type\text{-}specifier_{opt}\ initializable\text{-}declarator\text{-}list_{opt}\ ;$$

which is similar to the analogous external name declaration, except that there are four possible attributes controlling the visibility, lifetime, and storage class of variables. The **auto**matic attribute, which is the default, indicates that a variable is only visible within the compound statement most immediately enclosing its declaration and that on each separate execution of the compound statement, previous values of the variable will have been forgotten. The **register** attribute has the same meaning as **auto**matic and additionally has a request to keep the variable in high-speed registers normally available on general-purpose computers. Any initialization of **auto**matic or **register** variables is performed at each normal **entry** to the compound statement. Transfer of control (via **goto** or **switch**) into the middle of a compound statement bypasses this initialization.

64

The **static** attribute implies visibility only within the most immediately enclosing compound statement while the value of a **static** variable endures between separate executions of the compound statement. Any initialization is performed once, before program execution begins (possibly at compile-time). The **external** attribute indicates that all subsequent occurrences of the name in the current compound statement are taken to refer to an external declaration or definition for the name. It is good practice to explicitly import all external references used in a function. Initialization of an external variable at the site of a local declaration is not allowed.

Unlike external declarations, either the storage class or the type specifier must be present in a local declaration. Local declarations inside a block are terminated by the first statement that is not a local declaration.

The following ridiculous example illustrates these various possibilities:

```
int n = 0;    /* external by default */
static x;     /* only visible in current program-file */
extern float y[3] = {-1.0, 1.0, 0.0};
glob ( )
      {
      float q;       /* automatic known only in glob */
      int *iptr = &n;      /* refers to external n */
      extern float y[ ];    /* can't initialize here */

      while (*ipstr != '\0')
            {
            static int count;           /* count and ch */
            register char ch = 'A';     /* only known here */

            if (*ipstr == ch)
                  return(count);
            ++count;         /* ch dies each time */
            ++ipstr;         /* around loop, */
            }                /* but count lives on */
      ...
      }
```

A variable with the attribute **auto**matic or **register** that is not initialized will have an undefined value (i.e., garbage) at the start of execution of the compound statement. This is in contrast to **static** or externally declared variables, whose default initialization is to zero.

It is legal to redeclare a name local to a compound statement that already has a declared meaning by virtue of an external declarator (a declaration in an enclosing compound statement). Throughout the inner context (compound statement), the name will have the more locally declared meaning and, subsequent to this inner context, its meaning reverts to the more global meaning. The following example shows how this works:

```
int n;
float x;
main ( )
    {
    if (n > 0)                  /* global n */
        {
        char x = 'A';
        printf("%c", x);        /* local x char */
        }
    x = -1.0 / 2.5;             /* global x float */
    }
ff(int n;)                      /* argument is implicit local */
    {
    printf("%d", n);            /* not the global n */
    }
```

Note that a formal argument name constitutes an implicit local declaration.

The expressions used in initializers for locally declared **automatic** or **register** variables should include only those variables that are currently declared and have a value. Within the compound statement defining the body of a function, the arguments may be considered as having a defined value and so may be used to initialize local variables of the function body. For example,

```
float z = 1.0;
what(int a; char b;)
    {
    float x = a/z;
    int q = b&0377;
    float *fptr = &z;
    ...
    }
```

By special dispensation, formal arguments to a function may be given the storage class **register**. This does not imply that the corresponding argument necessarily is passed in a fast **register**, but that it is copied to one, if available, upon entry to the function for subsequent use. As with all uses of the **register** storage class, this should be considered as an *advice* to the compiler to help it better optimize code. It can never *cause* a diagnostic if there are insufficient (or no) registers available for allocation.

Register variables behave much as any **auto**matic variable, except that it is not permissible to take the address of a register; this means that they cannot be used with the unary **&** or binary . operators, and that they cannot hold composite items (arrays, structures, unions, functions).

4.1 Local integer variables

Integer variables may be locally declared with any of the storage classes **auto**, **register**, **static**, or **extern**. The first two may be initialized with any expression that is defined on entry to the compound statement and that may be assigned to an integer variable. The **static** locals follow the same rules as for external declarations [2.1]; **externs** may not be initialized.

4.2 Local floating point variables

Floating variables may be locally declared with any of the storage classes **auto**, **register**, **static**, or **extern**. The first two may be initialized with any expression that is defined on entry to the compound statement and that may be assigned to a floating variable. The **static** locals follow the same rules as for external declarations [2.2]; **externs** may not be initialized.

4.3 Local pointer variables

Pointer variables may be locally declared with any of the storage classes **auto**, **register**, **static**, or **extern**. The first two may be initialized with any expression that is defined on entry to the compound statement and that may be assigned to an integer variable. The **static** locals follow the same rules as for external declarations [2.3]; **externs** may not be initialized.

Note that there are many opportunities to assign the address of an **auto**matic variable to a pointer in such a way that the pointer outlives the thing to which it points. There is no check for this situation, and only sporadic hardware protection against subsequent use of invalid pointers. *Caveat emptor.*

4.4 Local arrays

Array variables may be locally declared with any of the storage classes **auto, static,** or **extern**. The **register** requests will not be honored. Nor can an **auto** array be initialized in the local declaration; an explicit loop or series of assignments must be coded. The size of a local array must be known at compile-time.

The **static** arrays are initialized following the same rules as in those presented [2.4].

4.5 Local structures and unions

Structure or union variables may be locally declared with any of the storage classes **auto, static,** or **extern**. The **register** requests will not be honored. Nor can an **auto** structure or union be initialized in the local declaration; explicit assignments must be coded.

The **static** structures and unions are initialized following the same rules as in [2.5].

4.6 Local function declarations

Functions may be locally declared with no storage class or with the storage class **extern** or **static**; any other declaration is illegal. The absence of a storage class is taken as **extern**, not **auto** as for all other local declarations. If a function is not declared, it is taken as a function returning integer. If any of its arguments is not declared, the corresponding actual parameter follows the default coercion rules given in [3.6].

A local function declaration is simply an indication to the compiler that the name in the local context is intended to refer (via calls) to an externally defined function of the identical name.

It is not permissible to define a function inside another function.

4.7 Local declaration syntax

The syntax of local declarations is

> *local-declaration* =
>   [**auto**$_{def}$ | **static** | **extern** | **register**]$_{opt}$
>   *type-specifier*$_{opt}$ *initializable-declarator-list*$_{opt}$;

where at least one each of storage class and type specifier must be present. Only scalar items may be initialized. Uninitialized items contain garbage.

5: PARAMETERS

*Merely corroborative detail, intended to give
artistic verisimilitude to an otherwise bald
and unconvincing narrative.*

— W.S. Gilbert, *Mikado*

5.0 The preprocessor

Before they are compiled, C programs are fed to a preprocessor, which makes textual substitutions under the influence of
explicit directives supplied as *control lines* in the text. Each control line begins with a # in column 1 of a line of source text.

The simplest forms of control line are simple definitions of
the form

> **#define** *identifier* {*token*}

or

> **#include** *file-name*

For example,

> **#define SIZE_LIMIT 10**

causes subsequent occurrences of the identifier **SIZE_LIMIT** to
be replaced by the constant **10**, while

> **#include my_macros**

causes the immediate inclusion of the file named **my_macros**
into the source text. Included files may contain other control
lines and the sequence of tokens replacing a defined identifier is

itself subject to replacements, and so on. For example, if file **lib1** contains lines

```
#include  defs
#include  mylib
```

and file **defs** is

```
#define  NMAX     10
#define  NEXTCH  getchar( )
#define  NMAX2    2*NMAX
```

and file **mylib** is

```
char cha[NMAX], matrix[NMAX, NMAX2];
for (i = 0 ; i < NMAX ; ++i)
      cha[i] = NEXTCH;
```

then the line

```
#include  lib1
```

will eventually be replaced by

```
char cha[10], matrix[10, 2 * 10];
for (i = 0 ; i < 10 ; ++i)
      cha[i] = getchar( );
```

It is now possible to redefine **NMAX** and **NEXTCH** by changing the first two lines in the file **defs** to

```
#define  NMAX      5
#define  NEXTCH  upper_case(getchar( ))
```

whereupon, without touching **mylib**, this modification is propagated by recompilation through the text of **mylib**. If the function **upper_case** did not exist originally on any of the included libraries, then it must somehow be so included, but **mylib** (which may be quite large) need not be modified directly.

Compiler diagnostics remain keyed to the original source line numbers even in the presence of **#include** statements. In fact, all diagnostics peculiar to an included file are given the line number of the **#include** statement.

5.1 Integer parameters

It is common convention to use uppercase letters to name *parameters* and all lowercase letters to name variables in a C program. It is good practice to **#define** all numbers in source code other than an occasional zero or one. Many zeros and ones, it should be pointed out, actually are the mystical values "no" and "yes," and should be labeled as such.

Each program file must **#include** a standard parameter file in order to achieve adequate source code control on even middling projects.

5.2 Floating parameters

Values such as *e* and π are excellent candidates for **#define** statements, as are the following: the number of digits worth keeping for **float** and for **double**; the largest number that can be safely inverted; and the smallest number that can be added to 1.0 and cause it to get bigger. While there are many things to watch for in writing floating point arithmetic that is truly portable, these parameters go a long way toward that goal.

5.3 Pointer parameters

The expression **&a[MAX−1]** is long-winded but useful. It often is worthwhile to parameterize as follows:

```
#define  MAX  100
#define  MAXP &a[MAX−1]

int a[MAX], *p;

for (p = a; p <= MAXP; ++p)
     < do p-th element >
```

Machine addresses used as pointers, as in machine-dependent device drivers, also benefit from proper mnemonics:

```
#define  CONSOLE  0177560

if ( CONSOLE −> status == DONE )
     resume( );
```

5.4 Array parameters

All array sizes should be parameterized with **#define**, if only to give mnemonic meaning to the chosen limit.

```
#define  MAXLINE  256
char   line[MAXLINE];
        for (i = 0; i < MAXLINE; ++i)
            putchar(line[i]);
```

Or, one can use the **sizeof** operator to advantage, as

```
#define  MAX  (sizeof a / sizeof a[0])
char a[10];

    for (i = 0; i < MAX; ++i)
        a[i] = '\0';
```

Note the use of parentheses in the **#define**, so that **MAX** may be used like any other term in an expression. The division by **sizeof a[0]** is necessary to convert from bytes to an element count. (See [3.1].)

5.5 Structure and union parameters

An elaborate structure declaration that is used throughout several program files is best kept in a parameter file — to be indicated by **#include** as needed. Unions are used almost exclusively, in fact, as a way of parameterizing multiple-use structures in a machine-independent fashion. (See [0.5].)

The **sizeof** operator can be used to read or write structures and unions in a highly portable fashion:

```
write (BINOUT, structure_a, sizeof structure_a);
```

5.6 Conditional compilation and arguments

Control lines also can be used for conditional compilation:

```
#ifdef PDP
        n++;
#else
        n--;
#endif
```

which is replaced by **n++**; if **PDP** is a currently defined identifier and otherwise is replaced by **n--**;. The control line

```
#ifndef PDP
```

means if **PDP** is not defined, use the following source lines, but it is otherwise the same as **#ifdef**. The **#else** may be omitted with the usual meaning.

Currently active definitions can be cancelled by control lines of the form

#undef *identifier*

after which this identifier will not be replaced until a subsequent definition occurs for this identifier. After such an undefinition, the identifier is considered undefined for purposes of the **#ifdef** or **#ifndef** control lines. For example,

```
#define N 2
        int a[N];
#undef N
        {float N; ... N = 1.3; ... }
#define N 4
        int k = 2 * N;
```

would finally become

```
        int a[2];
        {float N; ... N = 1.3; ... }
        int k = 2 * 4;
```

Note that definitions stack, so that a parameter may be **#define** over a short interval, then **#undef**, without affecting the usage of that parameter either before or after this interval.

A **#define** also may specify arguments for use when the definition is expanded. Thus,

```
#define swap(x,y) {int t; t=x; x=y; y=t}
```

behaves, for each invocation, as if

```
        swap (a,b)
```

were written as

```
#define x a
#define y b
        {int t; t=x; x=y; y=t;}
#undef a
#undef b
```

Note that in the definition the left parenthesis delimiting the argument list must be immediately adjacent to the defined identifier, or the list will be treated as part of a definition having no arguments.

5.7 Syntax

The complete syntax of preprocessor control is given by the following rules:

program-file =
    {*line-group*}

line-group =
    [{*source-line*} | *control-group*]

control-group =
    [**#define** *name* {*token*}
    | **#define** *name* (*arg-list*) {*token*}
    | **#include** *file-name*
    | **#**[**ifdef** | **ifndef**] *name*   {*line-group*}
    (**#else** {*line-group*})$_{opt}$
    #endif
    ]

6: PROGRAM LIBRARY

I can call spirits from the vasty deep.

Why so can I, or so can any man;
but will they come when you do call for them?

— Shakespeare, *King Henry IV*

6.0 Introduction

Since the C language proper does not include any input-output facilities, a viable environment must include at least a basic set of I/O functions. This chapter will describe these input-output facilities, as well as other standard functions frequently used or of such a nature that the user could not create them in C itself (e.g., exit to system).

6.1 Integer natural functions

The most basic requirement for input-output is the opening and closing of named files. The function **copen** has the "virtual" declaration.

```
int copen (char file_name[ ], access_mode[ ]; int record_size);
```

Given a **file_name** identifier and an **access_mode** indicator ("r", "w", "a", for read, write, or append), **copen** will return a "file descriptor" usable in other I/O calls to specify the active file. File descriptors are small positive integers. The **file_name** already should exist in the environment's file system whenever read access is requested. If write or append are requested for a nonexistent **file_name**, then a new file is created (and presumably entered into the file system). Incorrect use of **copen** is signaled by a return value less than zero.

76

The **record_size** argument is optional. It is needed on some systems when opening files for "direct," i.e., random, access. In this case, the convention is to create the file with mode **"ad"** and specified **record_size**, then to later read it with mode **"ad"** and the same size.

The file is closed by a call

    cclose(fd)

where **cclose** has the virtual declaration

    int cclose(int fd);

and accomplishes the disassociation of the file descriptor **fd** from the externally named file to which it was associated by the previous **copen** call. Once again, a negative return indicates that the operation failed.

The C run-time environment provides three standard files for input, output, and error messages referenced by the file descriptors:

    #define   STDIN   0
    #define   STDOUT   1
    #define   ERROUT   2

The first two are associated normally with a user's remote terminal, but may be redirected; the latter almost always is associated with the terminal, for error reporting. None of these files need be opened or closed by the user, and there exist I/O functions that read from **STDIN** or write to **STDOUT** by default.

The two functions **getc** and **putc** have virtual declarations:

    int getc(int fd;);
    int putc(int fd, c;);

the first, **getc**, returning the next character of file **fd** or **EOF**, which has the value −1, if end-of-file **fd**. Calls to **getc** advance the file position past the character returned. In addition, the function **backc** with virtual declaration

    int backc(int fd, c;);

puts back character **c** onto the current front of the file **fd** so that the next call to **getc** will obtain the character put back. Successive calls to **backc** without an intervening call to **getc** are disallowed — the put-back stack being of size one. Both **putc** and **backc** return the character sent, a convenience for writing expressions.

Note that the characters transmitted by these functions are implemented as **ints**. This permits **EOF** to be defined as a value that cannot be mistaken for a valid character.

For the convenience of programmers who frequently use the standard files **STDIN** and **STDOUT**, the functions **getchar** and **putchar** are provided:

```
getchar( )      ≡      getc(STDIN)
putchar(c)      ≡      putc(STDOUT, c)
```

and so are equivalent to **getc** and **putc** with defaults for the file descriptors.

6.2 Floating functions

The function **sqrt** has virtual declaration:

```
double sqrt(double x;);
```

and delivers a suitably precise approximation to the square root of a nonnegative floating value **x**. The result is undefined for negative **x**.

6.3 Pointers

To provide for dynamic storage allocation needed to implement linked data structures, the functions **calloc** and **cfree** are supplied with virtual declarations:

```
char *calloc(int number, size_in_bytes;);
cfree(char *p;);
```

The function **calloc** returns a pointer value that refers to the start of an untyped object in the memory, of size (**number * size_in_bytes**), which can be manipulated by the program owning the pointer value until the object is freed by a call to **cfree** with the same pointer value as argument. It is expected that **calloc** and **cfree** will be used to obtain and free rather large hunks of object-space, which will be chopped up and storage-managed by a user program.

The following example illustrates one possible approach:

```
typedef struct node {struct node *n[3]; char color[ ];} NODE;
typedef NODE *NODE_REF;
typedef union {NODE nd; NODE_REF link;} EXTNODE;
static EXTNODE *next_avail;
make_avail(int num;) /* make space available for num NODEs */
        {
        int k;
        EXTNODE *p1, *p2;

        next_avail = p1 = calloc(num, sizeof(EXTNODE));
        for (k = 1; k < num; ++k)
                {
                p2 = p1 + 1;
                p1 -> link = p2;
                p1 = p2;
                }
        p1 -> link = NULL;
        /* next_avail points to linked list of num NODEs */
        }

new(NODE_REF *ndr;) /* get new NODE pointed at by ndr */
        {
        *ndr = next_avail;
        if (next_avail != NULL)
                next_avail = next_avail -> link;
        }

free(NODE_REF *ndr;) /* *ndr rejoins available pool */
        {
        ndr -> link = next_avail;
        next_avail = ndr;
        *ndr = NULL; /* really free it ! */
        }
```

If the above constitutes a separate program file, then all access to the dynamic pool of **NODEs** is through calls to **make_avail**, **new**, and **free**. The type names **NODE** and **NODE_REF** are, of course, more globally known.

6.4 String input-output

Two functions, **gets** and **puts**, are provided to allow input and output of an entire array of characters. These functions have virtual declarations:

```
int gets(int fd; char line[ ]; int max_size;);
int puts(int fd; char string[ ]; int size;);
```

The function **gets** will fill character array **line** with successive characters from the front of file **fd** up to a maximum number specified by **max_size**. The returned value will be **NULL** if **EOF** is encountered on **fd**; otherwise, it will be an integer between 1 and **max_size** giving the number of characters actually read.

The function **puts** will append **size** characters of array **string** at the back of file **fd**. The value returned always should equal **size**; otherwise, a write error may be assumed.

6.5 Formatted input-output

Three functions **cprintf**, **sprintf**, and just plain **printf** are provided to allow the printing of character forms of numerical quantities. Their virtual declarations are

> **cprintf(int fd; char control[ ];** *arg-list* **);**
> **sprintf(char destination[ ]; char control[ ];** *arg-list* **);**
> **printf(char control[ ];** *arg-list* **);**

where *arg-list* is a variable-length sequence of arguments of unpredictable type, whose actual types in a call should match certain *out-control-items* in the actual argument corresponding to **control**. The function **printf** is simply **cprintf** with a default file **STDOUT** and **sprintf** is the same as **cprintf** except that the converted character array is placed into **destination** rather than being sent to a file.

The value of any character array used as an actual argument for **control** should consist of a sequence of *non-%-characters*, **%%**, or *out-control-items* whose syntax is

> *out-control-item* =
>   % *field-specification*$_{opt}$ *[* l *|* **L** *]*$_{opt}$
>   *out-conversion-specification*

field-specification =
　　　　− *opt*　% *left justification within field*

　　　minimum-field-width

　　　(. *subfield-size)opt*

minimum-field-width =
　　　{*digit*}

subfield-size =　　　% *fractional precision or*
　　　{*digit*}　　　　% *char array prefix size*

out-conversion-specification =
　　　[**d**　% *decimal notation*
　　　| **h**　% *short arg −> decimal*
　　　| **o**　% *unsigned octal (no leading 0)*
　　　| **x**　% *unsigned hexadecimal (no 0x)*
　　　| **u**　% *unsigned decimal*
　　　| **c**　% *character*
　　　| **s**　% *character sequence up to null char*
　　　　　　　% *or maximum subfield-size*
　　　| **e**　% *scientific notation for floating value*
　　　| **f**　% *whole . fraction notation*
　　　| **g**　% *the shorter of* **e** *or* **f**
　　　]

The arguments in the *arg-list* should match the control items as to number and type. For example, the call

```
printf("x= %f,k= %d,%s\n",x,k,"what?")
```

might cause printing of the following output line on **STDOUT**:

```
x=−3.140000,k=307,what?
```

whereas the call

```
printf("x=%−7.2f,k=%5d\n%−6.3s%%\n",x,k,"what?");
```

could print

```
x=−3.14 ,k=  307
wha %
```

Notice that %% represents the character %, not a control item header.

For formatted input, there are three analogous functions — **cscanf, sscanf,** and **scanf** — with virtual declarations

> **cscanf(int fd; char control[ ];** *arg-list* **);**
> **sscanf(char source[ ]; char control[ ];** *arg-list* **);**
> **scanf(char control[ ];** *arg-list* **);**

where *arg-list* is a list of pointers to unknown types.

The character array **control** must have the form

> { [*whitespace*   % *disregarded*
> | **%%** | *non-%-character*   % *must match input*
> | *in-control-item*]

where

> *whitespace* =
> { [*blank* | *newline* | *tab*] }
>
> *in-control-item* =
> % **ₒₚₜ*   % * *suppresses assignment*
> *maximum-field-width*ₒₚₜ
> *in-conversion-specification*
>
> *maximum-field-width* =
> {*digit*}
>
> *in-conversion-specification* =
> [**d**   % *decimal integer expected*
> | **o**   % *octal integer*
> | **x**   % *hexadecimal integer*
> | **s**   % *character sequence delimited by whitespace*
> | **c**   % *next character even if whitespace*
> | **d** | **f** % *floating constant*
> | [*^ₒₚₜ* {*non-]-char*}]
>   % *string of chars in the sequence*
>   % *or (when ^ present) not in the sequence*
>]

6.6 Exit

The **exit** function

```
int exit(int code;);
```

terminates the current process and delivers control to the process originally activating this process. The **exit** never returns. The argument **code** may or may not be used depending strongly on the operating system.

7: MACHINE DEPENDENCIES

7.0 Machine and system dependencies

This chapter is intended to cover those aspects of the current implementation of C (PDP-11 under RSX-11M or UNIX[†]) that are not defined in the portable part of the language but are defined or made more precise by the hardware of the PDP-11, or the operating system. These dependencies will be discussed in appropriate sections whenever possible, but the following list presents a general overview of topics, indicating where details can be found:

(1) hardware representation of basic types [7.1, 7.2, 7.3]

(2) hardware implementation of operators on basic types [7.1, 7.2]

(3) ASCII seven-bit characters in eight-bit bytes [7.1]

(4) restrictions on identifier length [7.0]

(5) treatment of external or global names and library conventions [7.0]

(6) widening, narrowing, and confrontations [7.1, 7.2, 7.3, 7.6]

(7) memory mapping of structures and unions [7.5]

[†] UNIX is a registered trademark of Bell Laboratories.

(8) order of evaluation [7.0, 7.6]

(9) arithmetic overflow and underflow [7.1, 7.2]

(10) defaults [7.1, 7.6]

(11) run-time environment; use of stack and frames; machine register usage; arguments and returns [7.1]

(12) treatment of the register attribute [7.0, 7.6]

One of the dependencies that users should be aware of from the start deals with external names: External names will be truncated to their first six characters (seven under UNIX), so they should differ one from another in the truncated form. Under RSX-11M, external names are presented to the loader with the underscore '_' replaced by '.'. Internal names are significant to 127 characters. Run-time support routines typically have a "c." prefix so that they cannot be called explicitly.

The compiler *does* exploit its freedom to chose the evaluation order of subexpressions except where the language defines the order. See [7.6] for the order of evaluation of arguments.

Within each function, up to three 16-bit registers are available to store integer values (**long int** needs two) and two 64-bit floating registers to store floating values. These registers can be commandeered by the **register** attribute in local declarations.

7.1 Binary integers

Characters are eight-bit two's complement binary integers, but the normal character set is the ASCII set of unsigned seven-bit values. The ASCII character set with hexadecimal equivalents and escape characters for often-used non-graphics is given by Table 7A. The collating sequence for ASCII corresponds to reading the columns left to right, and downward in each column. Each column identifier represents the first hexadecimal digit, while each row identifier represents the second. Boldface characters represent graphic (i.e., printable) characters which, in C programs, are enclosed between single-quote symbols. For example, the capital letter *zee* is written **Z** and represented as the eight-bit integer whose hex form is **0x5A**.

Table 7A
ASCII Characters and Hexadecimal Equivalents

	0	1	2	3	4	5	6	7
0	nul	dle	space	0	@	P	`	p
1	soh	dc1	!	1	A	Q	a	q
2	stx	dc2	"	2	B	R	b	r
3	etx	dc3	#	3	C	S	c	s
4	eot	dc4	$	4	D	T	d	t
5	enq	nak	%	5	E	U	e	u
6	ack	syn	&	6	F	V	f	v
7	bel	etb	'	7	G	W	g	w
8	bs	can	(	8	H	X	h	x
9	ht	em	)	9	I	Y	i	y
A	nl	sub	*	:	J	Z	j	z
B	vt	exc	+	;	K	[	k	{
C	np	fs	,	<	L	\	l	|
D	cr	gs	—	=	M	]	m	}
E	so	rs	.	>	N	^	n	~
F	si	us	/	?	O	_	o	del

Table 7B
Non-graphic Characters, Escapes, and Meaning

nul	\0	null char terminating strings
bs	\b	back space
ht	\t	horizontal tab
nl	\n	newline or linefeed
cr	\r	carriage return
ff	\f	formfeed or newpage
can	\30	cancel
space	b	blank or space

Character constants of more than one character will be truncated on the left when there is inadequate space for them. A two-character constant will occupy the left (high-order) and then right (low-order) byte of a plain **int**. For example, these two assignments are equivalent:

k = '?A';   k = 0x3F41;   /* k an int */

because ? corresponds to **3F** and A to **41**. Character constants may not be longer than 127 characters.

Plain and short integers are 16-bit or two-byte two's complement binary integers (refer to PDP-11 hardware manual), and **long int** is a 32-bit or four-byte two's complement binary integer. Unsigned integers are 16-bit simple unsigned positive binary integers module 2^{16}. The following table gives the ranges of values for the integer types:

char	−128 ...	+127
int (short)	−32,768 ...	+32,767
unsigned int	0 ...	+65,535
long int	−2,147,483,648 ...	+2,147,483,647

The integer arithmetic operators are those expected on a two's complement machine and the bitwise operators are standard except that >> fills the emptied bits on the left with the original left bit, which is the sign.

The rules for widening preserve the true integer value except that widening an **int** to an **unsigned int** causes no conversion of the binary representation and, hence, the negative **ints** will become effectively positive **ints** in the range 32,768 ... 65,535 (e.g., −1 becomes 65,535).

Whenever a wider integer value is assigned to an integer variable or argument that is narrower, the prefix is truncated; this rule preserves the integer value when the value is actually in the valid range for the narrower variable or argument, except for narrowing from **unsigned int** to **int** that is opposite to widening as described above.

Narrowing conversions from **float** or **double** to integer will preserve the sign and the whole part (truncating the fraction) if the integer target has adequate range. Note that **float** is considered to be *wider* than **long** even though it preserves fewer bits to the left of the radix. This normally should cause trouble only in 11/40 or LSI-11 floating points.

No overflow or underflow checking takes place in integer arithmetic; bits are set but no hardware interrupts are generated and no compiled code tests these exception bits.

• All non-character values occupy at least two bytes and, so, begin on a word (two-byte) boundary. This simply means the address of the first byte of the variable is an even integer location. The **chars** may begin at any byte address.

7.2 Binary floating point numbers

Values of type **float** or **short double** require 32-bits or four-bytes subdivided into a one-bit sign, an unsigned eight-bit exponent, and an unsigned 23-bit fraction with a suppressed leading one-bit. The exponent is encoded in *excess 128*-notation, which means that 128 corresponds to a base 2 power of 0, 129 to 1, 127 to −1, and so on. This gives a range of exponents from 10^{-38} to 10^{+38} approximately and somewhat over six decimal digits of precision. Values of type **double** or **long float** have an unsigned 55-bit fraction with approximately 16 decimal digits of precision and the same form and range of exponent.

Arithmetic on floating values is the standard normalized floating point arithmetic supported by PDP-11 hardware. Run-time routines are careful to preserve this form; for example, if the mantissa is zero, the entire number is set to zero.

Widening from **float** to **double** preserves values, as does **int** or **char** to **float** or **double**. Widening from **long int** to **float** may lose significant numerical information if the value of the **long int** exceeds 24 bits. The conversion from **long int** to **double** always preserves the correct value.

Narrowing from **double** to **float** loses the least significant digits of fractional precision. Depending on the instruction set option, rounding may or may not occur. As in the case of integer arithmetic, no overflow or underflow checking is performed. Floating values require a two-byte boundary.

It is assumed that, on entry to any C function, the arithmetic mode of the FPP is **double** (versus **float**) and **int** (versus **long**). These mode settings are preserved on exit from a C function. On 11/40s and LSI-11s with the floating option, **float** arithmetic is performed by the hardware instructions (see [7.6]). Any arithmetic options that are about are supported by in-line calls to run-time routines.

7.3 Pointer values

Valid byte addresses on the PDP-11 may range from one to 65,535 or 0x1 to 0xFFFF hexadecimal; zero has been reserved as the null pointer value. Hence, **unsigned int** is similar to the representation for pointers or location values.

Since all addresses are to byte-level, there is no checking of assignments between pointer types. This can cause trouble if a pointer to **char** is used as a pointer to **int**, since a bus error may result. The following assignments or implied assignments (actual to formal arguments) are allowed without any conversion of binary representation:

$$T_1\text{-pointer} \rightarrow T_2\text{-pointer}$$
$$\text{pointer} \rightarrow \text{integer}$$
$$\text{integer} \rightarrow \text{pointer}$$

The construction *int-expr* $->$ *part-name* also is allowed. Such deviations from normal type restrictions should be used judiciously. Pointer values are aligned on two-byte boundaries.

7.4 Arrays

Arrays are not assignable (as a unit) and may not appear as arguments or returned value of a function or with the **register** attribute.

Initialized array variables may have more than one unspecified range of valid subscripts if the first initializer row size gives the size required. For example,

        int k[ ][ ] = {{1,2,3}, {4}, {5,6}};

is tantamount to

        int k[3][3] = {{1,2,3}, {4,0,0}, {5,6,0}};

There is no promise that this will be portable, or always so for PDP-11s.

Arrays have the same boundary requirement as the element type from which the array is constructed. The **sizeof** an array is the **sizeof** its element type multiplied by the number of elements. For example,

double dbl[3][2];

has 48 bytes = (3 * 2 * 8).

String constants may be no longer than 127 characters.

7.5 Structures and unions

Like arrays, structures and unions are not assignable as units, may not appear as arguments or returned value of functions, and may not have the **register** attribute.

The mapping of structure parts into relative locations is done from left to right through the parts list with each part aligned as closely next to the end of the previous one as possible. This means there may be an occasional one-byte hole (i.e., an unused byte-location). For example, the declaration

struct {char ch; int k; char str[3];}

has the following layout:

| ch | hole | k | str | hole |
| | | | | | | | |

an initial boundary alignment of two-bytes and a **sizeof** = 8. The structure inherits the alignment of its most restricted part (here it is **k**), and **sizeof** is made to conform to the alignment so that structures of the same type will pack back-to-back with no holes — hence, the extra hole at the end of the above structure.

A union inherits the alignment of its most restrictive alternative part and a size equal to the maximum size among its parts adjusted so that unions pack back-to-back also.

7.6 Functions and run-time environment

Functions may not have arrays, structures, unions, or other functions as arguments or returned value, but pointers to same are allowed. In the absence of declarative information about argument types of a function, the compiler will assume **int** or **double** for an actual argument of type integer or floating respectively. Better control is attained when the programmer declares all known information about the argument and return types of external functions.

In particular, the 11/40 or LSI-11 floating point instructions can be used to maximum advantage only by declaring *explicitly* all floating quantities to be **float**. Otherwise, the compiler will call on run-time code to do many conversions to **double** in order to satisfy the default typing rules.

Actual argument expressions are calculated in reverse order to that specified in the call so that the run-time stack looks like

$$\text{arg}_n, \text{arg}_{n-1}, \ldots, \text{arg}_1, \text{return-link}$$

just before transfer to the function.

A typical use of the eight integer and four fully addressable **double** floating registers of the PDP-11 is as follows:

Integer Register

PDP-11 Value	Mnemonic	Meaning
0	R0	Integer return values
1	R1	or volatile values
2	R2	Integer free registers
3	R3	commandeerable
4	R4	by user
5	FP	Frame pointer for functions (R5)
6	SP	Stack pointer
7	PC	Program counter

Floating Register

PDP-11 Value	Mnemonic	Meaning
0	FR0	Floating return values
1	FR1	or volatile values
2	FR2	Floating free (!)
3	FR3	and commandeerable

In this register usage scheme, it would be the responsibility of each C function (whether compiler or user built!) to return to its caller with registers R2, R3, R4, FP, SP, FR2, and FR3 in the same state as obtained at entry to the function. Moreover, the mode bits of the FPP must be **double** and **int** as described in [7.0]. Returned values are expected as follows, depending on the type:

char, int, short int, unsigned int, pointer	R0
long int	R0/R1
floating, double	FR0

In machines that do not have a FPP, **floats** could be returned in R0/R1, and **double** results in a globally declared accumulator **c.fe**. The **c.fe** would behave exactly as **FR0**; i.e., it is assumed to be volatile in function calls and must be saved, along with other registers, to make code reentrant. There also would be a **c.fe** analogous to **FR1**, but there might not be any that is allocatable and that corresponds to **FR2** and **FR3**.

The condition codes are not assumed to be meaningful on return from any C function.

In most implementations, the compiler meticulously maintains a chain of stack frames, so that at any time

1) FP is the current frame pointer

2) 2(FP) is the return address from the most recent call

3) 0(FP) is the previous frame pointer

An exception to this would be any function compiled for the 11/40, LSI-11 floating point option. In this case, a possible implementation would be as follows:

1) FP is the current frame pointer

2) 6(FP) is the return address from the most recent call

3) 4(FP) is the previous frame pointer

4) 0(FP) is one floating accumulator

5) −4(FP) is the other floating accumulator

On top of this area of the stack frame are pushed

1)   registers R4, R3, R2

2)   sufficient space to hold the maximum number of **autos** ever used in the function

3)   and any other non-volatile register used by the function, either explicitly or implicitly

Thus, it is easy to trace a nesting of calls if the stack is intact. Note that return link information is most easily corrupted by the following:

1)   altering a nonexistent argument (expected but not passed)

2)   storing just outside an **auto** array

SUMMARY

Any programming language is an assemblage of various gadgets — literals, names, operators, expressions, declarations, array and structure constructors, functions, sequence control features, and so on. But this is an extremely limited point of view. As a tool for the construction of good programs, the language should support, and even encourage, the various methods now associated with good software engineering practices. Of primary importance are modularity, structured control, and systematic structuring of data.

True modularity means that the parts of a large program are relatively independent and that the dependencies are precisely documented. Certain details inside each part (program logic or data representation) are thereby hidden from the other parts. This practice of encapsulating details has been applied to program logic for some time now (i.e., subroutines) and more recently to data representations (i.e., data abstraction modules). The functions of C, with their formal arguments and locally declared data, support the encapsulation of program logic; separately compiled program files with minimum use of the external attribute support the encapsulation of data representation.

Structured control means a discipline of program logic dominated by sequence selection and repetition. To properly support this discipline, a language needs a general facility for grouping a sequence of statements into a unit. The compound statements of C provide for grouping, while the **if** and **switch** statements make selections; systematic control of repetitions is accomplished by the **while, do,** and **for** statements. Occasional needs for early termination of repetitions are catered for by **break**.

Systematic structuring of data includes multiples of like elements, composites formed from unlike elements, items that at any time may be one of several choices, and the ability to create access links between items of data. The arrays, structures, unions, and pointers of C do just that.

Besides the major issues just discussed, a program benefits greatly by being maintainable, portable, and efficient. Programs in C can be made more maintainable by use of defined parameters instead of literals, by use of macros [e.g., swap (a,b)] instead of replicated code, and through the definition of often-used data types (via **typedef**). Since most of the C language is independent of machine and operating system, programs in C can be very portable. Finally, the basic data types and operators of C are available directly in most machines, thus enabling quite efficient code to be generated.

The reader is encouraged to use this summary as an introduction to rereading *C Notes* — this time, viewing the language as a tool for good program design and practicing how to use it this way.

INDEX